IMPACTFUL
DEVELOPMENT
AND COMMUNITY
EMPOWERMENT

A Common Ground Monograph

IMPACTFUL DEVELOPMENT AND COMMUNITY EMPOWERMENT

Balancing the Dual Goals of a Global CLT Movement

John Emmeus Davis

Line Algoed

María E. Hernández-Torrales

EDITORS

TERRA NOSTRA PRESS

Madison, Wisconsin, USA

TERRA NOSTRA PRESS

Center for Community Land Trust Innovation
3146 Buena Vista Street
Madison, Wisconsin, USA 53704

Publisher's Cataloging-in-Publication Data

Names: Davis, John Emmeus, editor. | Algoed, Line, editor. | Hernández-Torrales, María E., editor.
Title: Impactful development and community empowerment : balancing the dual goals of a global CLT movement / John Emmeus Davis ; Line Algoed ; María E. Hernández-Torrales, editors.
Series: Common Ground Monographs
Description: Includes bibliographical references. | Madison, WI: Terra Nostra Press, 2021.
Identifiers: Library of Congress Control Number: 2021901598
ISBN: 978-1-7344030-9-1 (paperback) | ISBN: 978-1-7362759-0-0 (ebook)
Subjects: LCSH Land trusts. | Land tenure. | Land use. | Land use, Urban. | Nature conservation. | Landscape protection. | Sustainable development. | Economic development—Environmental aspects. | City planning—Environmental aspects. | Community development. | Urban ecology (Sociology) | BISAC POLITICAL SCIENCE / Public Policy / City Planning & Urban Development | LAW / Housing & Urban Development | BUSINESS & ECONOMICS / Development / Sustainable Development | SOCIAL SCIENCE / Sociology / Urban
Classification: LCC KF736.L3 W49 2020 | DDC 333.2—dc23

CONTENTS

FIGURES

Introduction
A Dual-Goal Model of
Community Development

John Emmeus Davis, Line Algoed,
and María E. Hernández-Torrales

It has been fifty years since the founding of New Communities Inc., an organizational prototype that is widely considered to have been the "first" community land trust (CLT). Established by African-American activists in Albany, Georgia as a vehicle for extending their struggle for political rights into the realm of economic rights,[1] New Communities combined collective ownership of land by a community-based, nonprofit corporation, individual ownership of housing, and the cooperative operation of agricultural and other commercial enterprises. A "new model for land tenure in America" was how this unusual hybrid was described in the first book about CLTs, published in 1972.[2]

Community land trusts have proliferated over the past five decades, multiplying within the United States and spreading beyond the model's country of origin. So many CLTs now exist in England, Europe, Canada and, increasingly, in the Global South that it is no longer accurate to characterize the CLT as distinctively "American." Nor is there a single, uniform "model" of what a CLT is and does. As its numbers have grown and as its footprint has widened, the model has changed. Today, there are many variations on the theme of "CLT classic."

What has not changed is the dynamic tension between impactful development and community empowerment that was baked into the structure and purpose of the CLT from the very beginning. The founders of New Communities Inc., as well as the founders of most CLTs that came after, were committed to improving the lives of people from races and classes who were being systematically excluded from the political and economic mainstream. CLT practitioners were convinced that community-led development on community-owned land, the strategy embodied in their "new model for land tenure," was especially suited to rebuilding human settlements to benefit the many, not the few, bending the arc of development toward more equitable access to affordable housing, food security, essential services, and economic opportunity.

For that to happen, however, a CLT must gain control over enough land-based assets to have an impact on its chosen locale. It has to possess sufficient financial resources and organizational capacity to acquire more and more parcels of land, to develop an increasing quantity of housing (and other facilities), and to serve as the permanent steward of those assets. At the same time as a CLT is endeavoring to expand its portfolio of real property, moreover, it is dedicated to expanding its social base—continuously organizing, informing, and involving members of its chosen community in guiding and governing the CLT itself. This is not development from above, dictated by a governmental body, a charitable investor, or a benevolent provider of social housing; it is development from below, directed by those who live and work in the place a CLT has determined to serve. Ownership and empowerment go hand-in-hand.[3]

Within the larger field of community development, these goals are routinely considered uncomfortable companions at best, and irreconcilable rivals at worst. Even within the smaller world of CLTs, there has continued to be a vigorous debate as to whether there exists an inevitable tradeoff between going to scale versus ceding control to the community served by a CLT.

That debate infuses the present monograph. A few of the volume's contributors favor one side or the other, tilting toward scale or control, but most portray the CLT as occupying a rhetorical and practical middle ground, where the model's dual goals are brought into balance. They agree, in effect, with the argument made by Thaden and Pickett in the opening chapter that "scale is not the enemy of community control; nor is community and resident leadership the enemy of scaling up the number of permanently affordable homes." As examples, Thaden and Pickett point to three CLTs that pay particular attention to performing this balancing act: the Dudley Street Neighborhood Initiative in Boston, the City of Lakes CLT in Minneapolis, and the Houston CLT in Texas.

Subsequent chapters offer detailed portraits of other CLTs going to scale without sacrificing a commitment to community. The story of the Champlain Housing Trust (CHT), one of the world's largest CLTs, is told by Brenda Torpy. CHT has assembled a diverse portfolio of over 3,000 units of permanently affordable housing in and around Burlington, Vermont, along with over 160,000 square feet of space in nonresidential buildings. Meanwhile, CHT has maintained a community membership of over 6,000 individuals who elect a majority of CHT's governing board.

In San Juan, Puerto Rico, another CLT has demonstrated that community control can be a basis for expanding a CLT's portfolio, not a barrier. Line Algoed, María E. Hernández-Torrales, Lyvia Rodriguez Del Valle, and Karla Torres Sueiro tell the story of the Caño Martín Peña CLT, which emerged out of an intensive process of community organizing and participatory planning within seven informal settlements. The Caño CLT has succeeded in acquiring over 272 acres of land on which roughly 1,500 households had lived for decades without having security of tenure for the sites beneath their dwellings. Now their homes are protected.

By comparison, the Urban Land Conservancy (ULC) in Denver and the proliferation of urban CLTs in Canada provide pictures of going to scale that are more complicated. Alan Gottlieb and Aaron Miripol document ULC's success in building a sizable portfolio of land, rental housing, and nonresidential buildings, while lacking a community-led board. Yet ULC has actively and diligently involved local residents in planning and designing every one of its major projects. More recently, ULC has added a "CLT committee" to its organizational makeup, consisting of representatives from various organizations that own buildings on lands leased from ULC.

For their chapter, Susannah Bunce and Joshua Barndt trace the evolution of two "generations" of community land trusts in Canada. Large-scale housing cooperatives in Toronto and Montreal developed thousands of units of housing during the1980s and1990s, the affordability of which was eventually secured by creating land trusts to own and to manage the underlying land. Since 2014, a "second generation" of community-based CLTs has emerged with a broader agenda of community control over local development and participatory democracy. This has resulted in a greater number of CLTs, but these newer organizations have not yet come close to producing as many units of permanently affordable housing as the earlier hybrids that combine cooperative housing with a land trust.

What is illustrated by the Urban Land Conservancy and by the Canadian CLTs is that "community control" can take multiple forms. Participation in governance is not the only mechanism for involving residents in the work of a CLT. Furthermore, there may be a sequence—or a seesaw—between building a sizable real estate portfolio and ensuring resident involvement. At different times in a CLT's organizational development—or at different periods in the development of a national network—one of a CLT's strategic goals may take precedence over another, at least temporarily.

Olivia Williams argues in her chapter, on the other hand, that the pendulum has swung too far in the single direction of going to scale—and is in danger of getting stuck there. She sees a pattern of CLTs steadily abandoning the movement's original commitment to community control, a consequence primarily of pandering to the priorities of outside funders. She urges CLTs to find new ways of supporting land acquisition and development without relying on external grants. John Emmeus Davis, for his part, expresses more confidence in the resiliency of CLTs in finding an equilibrium between competing goals—as long as the model itself is not dismembered. In his concluding chapter, he argues that combining the dual goals and multiple components of a CLT is not only possible, but necessary, if a CLT is to have a transformative impact on the place-based community it has chosen to serve. Rather than lamenting the tensions that inhere in this unusual model of community-led development on community-owned land, he lauds the "particular genius" of CLT practitioners who masterfully fashion these "pesky tensions" into something that is "equitably in synch and sustainably in balance."

All of the chapters in the present monograph, except for the essay contributed by Thaden and Pickett, were selected from *On Common Ground: International Perspectives on the Community Land Trust.* Published by Terra Nostra Press in June 2020, this collection of twenty-six original essays opened with an Introduction that described the distinctive features of the community land trust, while acknowledging the model's many variations. It also outlined the "common ground" that is shared by most CLT scholars and practitioners around the world. Those introductory remarks are repeated in the sections that follow.

WHAT'S IN A NAME?

Community land trusts are not all alike. Among the hundreds of CLTs that already exist or are presently being planned, there are numerous variations in how these organizations are structured, how their lands are utilized, how development is done, and how the stewardship of housing is operationalized. What is called a "community land trust" can vary greatly from one country to another, even from one community to another within the same country.

COMMUNITY
(Organization)

LAND
(Ownership)

TRUST
(Operation)

These distinctive features of ownership, organization, and operation, overlapping and interacting in a dynamic model of place-based development, became eventually known as the "classic" CLT. Almost as soon as nearly everyone came to agree on this particular conception and configuration of the community land trust, however, the model began to be modified in countless ways. Variations arose in every feature of the "classic" CLT, as practitioners in different places adapted it to fit conditions, needs, and priorities in their own communities or to fit customs and laws in their own countries.

This continuing process of innovation and adaptation has helped the CLT to spread across a disparate international landscape and to thrive in a range of settings. At the same time, the diversity of meanings attached to the model and the variety of ways in which CLTs are structured has introduced a degree of difficulty to the task of explaining exactly what a CLT might be. Today, there is ambiguity—even a dose of controversy—to be found in the description and implementation of every component.

Community. Throughout the world, most organizations that call themselves a CLT are committed to involving a place-based population in their activities, incorporating a participatory ethos into their organization's purposes, practices, and structure. People who live on the CLT's lands and those who live nearby are encouraged to become voting members of the organization. They are recruited to serve on its governing board.[4] They are invited to participate in shaping the uses and projects proposed by the CLT. Development is "community-led," along with the organization that initiates and oversees that development.

Ambiguity enters the picture because of the varying arrangements that CLTs employ in striving to engage and to empower their community. Controversy arises because some CLTs have dispensed with community altogether, causing critics to question whether they should even be considered a "real" CLT. The traditional model's distinctive features of ownership and operation might be present, but residents who are served by the program neither govern nor guide it; that is, "community" is missing from the organizational makeup of the entity doing development. Variations like these create perennial challenges for CLT advocates whenever they try to reach a consensus as to what deserves to be deemed a "community land trust."[5]

Land. The typical CLT is a nonprofit organization that removes land permanently from the marketplace, managing it on behalf of a place-based community while making it available for long-term use by individuals and organizations. Title to the buildings on a CLTs land, either those existing when the CLT acquired the land or those constructed later on, is held individually by any number of parties—homeowners, cooperatives, businesses, gardeners, farmers, etc. The underlying land is leased from the CLT by the buildings' owners.

This mixed-ownership arrangement blurs the legal and conceptual boundary between conventional categories of tenure, where real property is presumed to be one thing or the other. A community land trust messes up this tidy picture, for it is balanced half-way between the two extremes of *individual property,* owned and operated primarily for the purpose of promoting private interests; and *collective property,* owned and operated to promote a common interest. The CLT tilts toward the former in its treatment of buildings. It tilts toward the latter in its treatment of land, making the CLT a first cousin to cooperatives, cohousing, and various forms of communal, collective, and tribal land.

Although a CLT's lands are frequently and fairly characterized as "community-owned" or, in the parlance of the present volume, as "common ground," these landholdings are neither collectively nor cooperatively owned by the people living on them or around them. Title is held exclusively by the CLT. A community land trust is ownership for the common good, not ownership in common.[6]

There are places, however, where the separation of ownership is made difficult (or impossible) by quirks in the property laws of a particular country or by the quibbles of prospective funders. CLTs have sometimes been compelled, therefore, to retain ownership of buildings as well as the land or to relinquish ownership of both, while imposing long-lasting restrictions on the use and affordability of these properties. Another variation has been developed in Puerto Rico, where the Caño Martín Peña CLT holds the underlying land but uses a durable surface rights deed, rather than a ground lease, to provide security of tenure for people who own and occupy houses on the CLT's land. Some of these residents are living on sites their families have occupied for nearly a hundred years.

Trust. Although "trust" is part of their given name, CLTs have rarely been established as real estate trusts.[7] Most are NGOs—private, nonprofit corporations with a charitable purpose of meeting the needs of populations who are regularly underserved by both the market and the state. "Trust" refers not to how a CLT is organized, but to how it is operated. "Trust" is what a CLT does in overseeing the lands and buildings under its care and in performing the duties of stewardship. Foremost among these duties is the preservation of affordability, ensuring long-term access to land and housing for people of modest means and preventing their displacement due to gentrification and other pressures. Stewardship also includes such responsibilities as preventing deferred maintenance in housing and other buildings on the CLT's land and intervening, if necessary, to protect occupants against predatory lending, arbitrary eviction, mortgage foreclosure, and other threats to security of tenure. Some CLTs are focused less on the provision of housing, however, than on the preservation of watersheds, woodlands, or agricultural lands, either in rural or urban areas. The responsibilities of a CLT entrusted with managing such lands can look very different than the stewardship needed when affordable housing is a CLT's operational focus.

WHAT IS SHARED?

Despite this lack of uniformity in the description, implementation, and application of CLTs, there are commonalities nonetheless. What unites a global community of CLT scholars and practitioners is more important than what separates us. There is a *lingua franca* for understanding what it means for an organization to be a CLT and to behave like one. There is a shared commitment to reinventing and repurposing real estate for the common good. There is a shared conviction that community-owned land, in particular, is likely to do a better job of promoting equitable and sustainable development than land that is commodified and owned individually, especially in places populated by groups that have long been disadvantaged and disempowered.

Another trait that is shared by most CLT scholars and practitioners is a conviction that the whole of a CLT is greater than the sum of its parts. Across the diverse landscape of CLTs, ownership, organization, and operation are not configured exactly the same in every town and country. Wherever this strategy has been adopted, however, there is a general recognition that it takes more than a single component to make a CLT; it takes more than the reinvention of any one of them to bend the arc of development toward a fairer distribution of property and power. Community-owned land, by itself, is not enough. Community-led development is not enough. Permanently affordable housing is not enough. It is their *combination* that gives a CLT its distinctive identity and transformative potential.[8]

To be sure, there are places in the world where CLTs have been effective without adopting every feature of the "classic" CLT. That model is no longer a template, but it remains a touchstone. It is where most people start, when striving to adapt this complex form of tenure to their own situations. It is where most people hope a CLT will lead, when envisioning a better outcome from their arduous, virtuous labors, whether providing affordable housing, rebuilding residential neighborhoods, regularizing tenure in informal settlements, or preserving productive lands and local enterprises at risk of being lost to market pressures.

When land is owned for the common good of a place-based community, present and future; when development is done by an organization that is a creature of that community, rooted in it, accountable to it, and guided by it; when stewardship is deliberate, diligent, and durable . . . justice is more likely to be achieved. And more likely to last. That is the moral impetus and lofty promise of common ground.

Notes

1. Mtamanika Youngblood, who had participated as a youth in the early efforts to establish New Communities Inc., was interviewed many years later for a documentary about this pioneering CLT (*Arc of Justice: The Rise, Fall and Rebirth of a Beloved Community,* Open Studio Productions, 2016). On camera, she described the multiple purposes of this rural initiative: "The idea behind New Communities was to take civil rights one step further into economic independence and economic rights, using agriculture as an economic base."

2. International Independence Institute, *The Community Land Trust: A Guide to a New Model for Land Tenure in America* (Cambridge MA: Center for Community Economic Development, 1972).

3. This interweaving of ownership and empowerment was never far from the minds of the African-Americans who pioneered the first CLT. A brochure for New Communities, Inc., printed in the 1970s, described the purpose of a land trust in this way: "It is people holding land together as a community; it is 'people power,' the security of holding and

owning together the land which, through development and use, will bring them the power to stand on their own two feet."

4. Organizationally, the model promoted by the Institute for Community Economics during the 1980s had an open membership and a three-part board, representing the interests of the people who live on the CLT's land, people who live within the CLT's service area, and institutions that served that geography, including government, churches, banks, businesses, and other NGOs. See Institute for Community Economics, *The Community Land Trust Handbook* (Emmaus PA: Rodale Press, 1982).

5. To a certain degree, we sidestepped this definitional debate in *On Common Ground* (2020) by featuring among the book's twenty-six chapters a number of organizations that self-identify as a community land trust, even if they do not exhibit every feature of what is known in the USA as the "classic" CLT. Our ecumenical embrace had limits, however. We admitted to the company of CLTs only organizations that were committed to removing land permanently from the stream of commerce, placing it under the ownership or control of a designated community and stewarding that land for the common good.

6. This echoes the earliest description of the CLT: "The community land trust is not primarily concerned with common ownership. Rather, its concern is ownership for the common good, which may or may not be combined with common ownership." International Independence Institute (1972), *op cit.*, page 1. Although the people living on a CLT's land do not hold title to the underlying land, the resale formula used by some CLTs does provide for a modest increase in the homeowner's equity if the land has appreciated in value during the homeowner's tenure.

7. Trusts are established by individuals to control the distribution of their property, either during their lifetimes or after their death. Property is often real estate, but it may also be stocks, bonds, or other income-generating assets. The person who creates the trust is called the "settlor." The person who holds the property for another's behalf is the "trustee." The latter takes title to the property, although under a "revocable trust" the settlor may later reclaim ownership. Proceeds from the trust are distributed by the trustee to a specific list of beneficiaries named by the settlor when the trust was established.

8. An argument for CLTs being more than the sum of their parts can be found in John Emmeus Davis, "Better Together: The Challenging, Transformative Complexity of Community, Land, and Trust," the final chapter in the present monograph.

1.

Community Land Trusts
Combining Scale and Community Control to Advance Mixed-Income Neighborhoods

Emily Thaden and Tony Pickett

Community land trusts (CLTs) continue to gain ground as an innovative model for achieving permanently affordable housing through community control of the land placed in trust. Large-scale implementation of the CLT model can buffer the adverse effects of systemic racism and involuntary displacement through gentrification, by ensuring that a lasting stock of high-quality, affordable housing remains in place to intentionally benefit communities of color, even when new investments create a market-driven increase in real estate values. When CLTs control a sufficient percentage of housing in areas that are high-cost or where housing costs are rising, the neighborhood can achieve mixed-income status. This has potential to enrich residents' lives across all income levels through diverse interconnectedness and opportunities for betterment.[1]

However, research continues to reveal just how challenging it is for mixed-income communities to produce benefits for lower-income people of color. Too often, communities of color that experience new investments, accompanied by an influx of more affluent and often predominately white households, report that the changes work to the benefit of the higher-income white households and the detriment of lower-income households of color. Residents of color are experiencing racism, including social and cultural alienation and a loss of political influence, which are often expressed in sentiments such as, "This is no longer my neighborhood." The CLT model, when focused with a racial equity lens, attempts to address both the perception and the reality of these shifts in power and culture by placing the residents of homes on the CLT's land in key leadership and decision-making positions and by putting the needs of low-income Black and Brown residents at the center of the CLT's mission.

A major debate among CLT practitioners and advocates involves the tradeoffs and tensions between "going to scale" with the housing portfolio and enacting "community control." People on one side of this debate make the case that increasing the number of homes held in trust is necessary, both for CLTs' financial sustainability and for the production and preservation of mixed-income, racially inclusive communities. The other side argues that ever-increasing scale may inevitably erode the community's and local residents' control in decision making—a vital part of the CLT governance model. As a recent publication on transformative land strategies argues, the evolution of CLTs has reached an "inflection point" and "scale is not an adequate end-goal if the commitment to the practice of democratic governance, and the organizing and political education to support it, are left by the wayside."[2]

In this essay, we suggest that pitting the straw men of scale and community control against one another does the field more harm than good. Instead, we support a theory of change that reconciles and balances the two goals in order to create more comprehensive CLT-based approaches that advance racial justice and inclusive community development. The non-violent protests in Albany, GA during the 1960s— which were an instrumental part of the Black-led Civil Rights movement— gave birth to the CLT model. And today, the global protests of the Black Lives Matter movement set forth demands for racial justice and radical solutions to address systemic social, political, and economic exclusion of Black and Brown people and their communities. These demands call out CLTs as a vehicle to transform land use and housing through community control of both. This is, indeed, an inflection point for CLTs. We must center ourselves in our Civil Rights history and fight harder than ever to realize our transformational racial justice work through CLTs. But to begin, we must first explain the CLT model and its challenges.

AFFORDABLE HOUSING IN MIXED-INCOME COMMUNITIES DONE DIFFERENTLY: THE CLT MODEL

Unfortunately, the majority of new affordable housing developed in urban areas follows an ill-fated pattern:[3] Public funds are invested to improve disinvested communities, address poor housing conditions, and create high-quality affordable housing options. Improvements to the affordable housing stock often spur additional private real estate investments within the same area. The neighborhood is considered to be "revitalizing"— an unmanaged process that may slowly or quickly turn into gentrification. Higher property values drive up rents and property taxes, which attracts higher-income households and more private investment. This begins to push out lower-income households. Additional displacement pressure often occurs as the affordability periods for the affordable housing stock start to expire and properties revert to market-rate.[4] When that happens, residents of the affordable housing also get displaced.

Within this pattern there is a brief period—somewhere between revitalization and gentrification—when the community is mixed-income and, typically, more racially diverse. However, this period quickly wanes in the absence of stopgaps to prevent the pressure of displacement. Ultimately, the neighborhood may end up more segregated than it was before public investment hit the streets. CLTs provide a solution to this unanticipated consequence of development. Community land trusts are nonprofit corporations that steward community assets and provide permanently affordable housing for families and communities. CLTs acquire and secure land with a renewable ground lease (typically with a 99-year agreement) and ensure that all affordable housing on that land remains affordable in perpetuity. If CLTs can create a significant stock of affordable housing in neighborhoods, they act as bulwarks against gentrification and low-income resident displacement.

CLTs and "Community Control"

In his framework of displacement, Dan Immergluck defines political displacement as occurring when new residents belonging to racial and economic groups that have traditionally held more power move into a neighborhood and stifle the voice of long-time residents, which perpetuates economic and racial supremacy.[5] CLTs mitigate this type of displacement by placing current and future lower-income residents at the center of "community control" and decision making about neighborhood needs. Unlike most other nonprofits or community development corporations, the traditional CLT governance model operationalizes community control by being structured as a nonprofit, corporate-community membership organization whose members include all residents of CLT homes and other residents in the CLT service area. The members pay nominal annual dues and support the CLT's mission. Members have decision-making authority over major decisions.

Fast Facts About CLTs

- The first CLT, New Communities, Inc., was established in Albany, GA in 1969 by local civil rights leaders to benefit African-American farmers who desired to advance their racial justice agenda for economic empowerment by gaining collective control over farmland and housing.

- In 2018, Grounded Solutions Network estimated that there are approximately 225 CLTs in 46 states and the District of Columbia. Of those, about 60 organizations are start-ups or have no housing units. Roughly 165 CLTs have homeownership units, totaling approximately 12,000 homes. Many CLTs also have affordable rental portfolios, estimated to include 25,000 rental units.

One-third of a traditional CLT's board of directors is elected by and composed of residents living on the CLT's land, and an equal portion is elected by and composed of members who reside within the CLT's targeted "community" but do not live on the CLT's land. This structure balances the interests of residents of different incomes, races, cultures, and backgrounds to ensure that the uses of CLT-owned land prioritizes the needs of all members.

Through their commitment to community control, CLTs foster engagement and interconnectedness among economically and racially diverse residents to enact the CLT's mission and decide on the prioritized uses of land owned in perpetuity by the CLT. Many CLTs also actively engage the communities where they hold land in trust through community events, educational programming, and opportunities for civic engagement.

CLTs and Homeownership

Depending on what the community needs, CLTs can develop rural and urban agriculture projects, commercial spaces to serve local communities, affordable rental and cooperative housing projects, or conserve land or urban green spaces. To date, however, most CLTs have focused mainly on creating homes that remain permanently affordable and thus provide successful homeownership opportunities for generations of lower-income families and families of color. The importance of this focus cannot be understated. Redlining, predatory lending, and other barriers have made homeownership through the private housing market incredibly difficult for lower- income families and households of color to attain and sustain. One study found that the probability of sustaining homeownership for longer than five years by first-time homebuyers who were low-income or people of color was equal to a fifty-fifty coin toss—and that was before the foreclosure crisis.[6]

By contrast, the approach used by CLTs, shared equity homeownership, invests public resources to reduce the home's initial price and then keeps the price affordable to all future homebuyers through resale restrictions. This gives the CLT a vested interest in the property and in the homeowner's success. Homes are not treated as risky and speculative investments; rather, homes are stabilizing and transformational forces. In return, the homeowners agree to sell their homes at a resale-restricted and affordable price to another lower-income homebuyer in the future. This arrangement enables the resident to own a home and build some wealth, and also enables the CLT to preserve the public's investment in making homes permanently affordable for family after family.

Evidence of CLT Effectiveness

CLTs have demonstrated effectiveness in increasing racial diversity and affordability; stabilizing the average household income in their neighborhoods; and maintaining middle-class ratios, education levels, and owner-occupied housing rates. Researchers have found, for instance, that:

▪ Homeowners in CLTs across the USA were 10 times less likely to be in foreclosure proceedings and eight times less likely to be seriously delinquent than homeowners across all incomes in the private market at the peak of the foreclosure.[7] Unlike many of their private-market counterparts, these residents were not displaced from their homes or their neighborhoods.

▪ Across 124 CLT neighborhoods in 15 states, community land trusts moderated the adverse effects of gentrification between 2000 and 2010 by increasing affordability, stabilizing housing prices, and reducing displacement, compared with similar non-CLT neighborhoods.[8] Moreover, even when gentrification is not the threat, CLTs foster a mixed-income community that grants access to opportunity and creates a thriving neighborhood for residents with modest incomes.[9]

▪ In a study of 58 shared equity homeownership programs and 4,108 properties over the past three decades, shared equity homes are: (1) serving low-income homebuyers and increasingly serving people of color, (2) providing affordable homes and mortgages, (3) ensuring homeownership is sustainable, (4) building wealth for families, (5) remaining permanently affordable to serve households of the same income levels over subsequent sales, and (6) retaining the public investment in affordable housing.[10]

These findings suggest that CLTs' affordable housing can withstand skyrocketing property values, land speculation, and the influx of higher-income households—making CLTs one of the best ways to stabilize neighborhoods, preserve affordability, and build community assets in neighborhoods.

If CLTs are delivering on their promises, then why aren't they proliferating? Lack of available funding is undoubtedly the biggest problem: Affordable housing requires that homes be subsidized to a below-market-rate price, and federal funds for rehabilitation and construction are hardly growing while costs are. In this essay, however, we want to focus on another challenge that is more in our collective control to change: the false dichotomy of community control, as represented by the CLT approach, versus getting to scale.

MEET THE STRAW MEN: "COMMUNITY CONTROL" VERSUS "SCALE"

In the debate over whether CLT practitioners and advocates should focus on community or scale, one side says that holding considerable land in trust, containing a large number of affordable homes, is antithetical to community control. The other side insists that the time needed to cultivate real community control is a barrier to achieving scale. Grassroots groups that focus solely on community control tend to minimize efforts to build the resource systems and infrastructure that CLTs need to develop and grow their impact (e.g., enabling public policies, a pipeline of real estate assets, and financing) because these activities are perceived as removed from the communities the groups are trying to serve. Conversely, groups that focus solely on scale tend to minimize community organizing and planning, resident empowerment, community ownership, and authentic place-based leadership of the CLT. The former approach fails to achieve the accumulation and development of enough land to foster mixed-income, racially diverse communities, and the latter approach fails to achieve enough resident empowerment and decision making to ensure that cultural and political displacement are prevented.

Two trends in current CLT development efforts exacerbate the debate. One is that more and more grassroots community groups are interested in bringing CLTs to their communities. These grassroots efforts often are highly effective at organizing the community and garnering resident-driven plans for the CLT, but they rarely succeed in obtaining land and bringing development to fruition; when they do, it is often as a one-off small development, or the CLT ekes out a couple of homes per year. In these cases, the community organizers often misconstrue the CLT model as "operating outside of the market" or want their CLT to subvert capitalism. They don't accept the fact that developers, government staff, and real estate and housing investors are vital partners for obtaining land, funding, and financing CLT community assets—just as they are for all affordable housing development—or they fear that scaling the CLT will mean sacrificing neighborhood-based decision making. Ironically, this stance can result in community residents losing the ability to control neighborhood land, and the disappointment and distrust that follows may (unjustly) be attached to the CLT concept rather than its implementation.

Another trend is that some CLTs are being successfully established as "programs" operated by nonprofit organizations. Sometimes these programs are adept at obtaining land and producing affordable housing, but they lack meaningful community control and resident authority because they are not governed by a corporate community membership and do not have community residents and leaseholders on their boards. Because the parent nonprofit has other lines of business and existing bylaws that compete for representative governance, community control of the CLT gets scant attention, or superficial community engagement is deemed sufficient. In the worst cases, a nonprofit takes the paternalistic or racist stance that facilitating authentic community control would hinder the pace of developing and scaling up the CLT program.

A RECONCILED APPROACH: SCALING UP COMMUNITY CONTROL

We argue that scale is not the enemy of community control; nor is community and resident leadership the enemy of scaling up the number of permanently affordable homes. Without community buy-in and accountability, the resources and will to scale up will not persist, which in turn means that permanently affordable homes are unlikely to be created and preserved.

Land is power, and people united is power. Reverend Charles Sherrod, a founder of the CLT model, impresses this point in the documentary film *Arc of Justice,* which chronicles the origins of the CLT model.[11] But Sherrod also shared his personal experience of "deep guilt and frustration" for inadvertently contributing to the suffering of Black families in rural communities. Many Black families were evicted from their homes and farms in rural Georgia as retaliation for Sherrod's work with them around the Student Non-Violent Coordinating Committee, organizing Black tenant farmers to exercise their right to vote. This unjust involuntary displacement from home and land was the impetus for developing New Communities, Inc. as the first CLT and transforming land tenure arrangements to a model of Black collective control.[12] Sadly, his personal trauma of feeling powerless to prevent the mass displacement of Black families is similar to frustrations articulated by contemporary CLT leaders' recently documented by MIT CoLab:

> Multiple people we interviewed expressed frustration that they could not do more to deliver for their people. "Do not tell these people that you're going to have housing built for them any time soon. Do not," Adrian from SMASH said. Zach from Oak CLT told us, "It's a frustration as a Black person to be in a space where we provide housing and have no ability to provide housing to the tens and hundreds of Black people I know who have an immediate need for housing. And these are all good folks, you know? That's a trauma that a Black person in this space has to live under. And it's not recognized.[13]

This deep personal trauma experienced by Black and Brown housing leaders attempting to serve millions of people of color in need must be healed by furthering justice. Hence, we need to urgently adopt a reconciled approach that advances both control of land at scale and democratic community decision making to achieve gains for Black and Brown residents, neighborhoods, cities, and society. Under a CLT approach that gives equal priority to community control and impact from scale, the systems and structures of land use policy and the housing finance and real estate industries may be fully utilized, so that communities can gain land in trust and hold CLTs accountable to their mission when scaled.

A reconciled approach, which specifically avoids being race neutral in its priorities and outcomes, holds the most promise for significantly impacting communities by holding racial and economic justice and integration at the heart of the CLT. Fundamentally, grassroots activists of color are best suited for community organizing and campaigning for political will, resources, and enabling policies that will support consistent and meaningful growth of the CLT's land holdings and affordable housing. Nonprofits that either are CLTs or have CLT programs should be doubling down on applying a racial equity lens and gaining community control of land so it can be leveraged into community buy-in and leadership for advocacy, vital ingredients for reaching scale. Put differently, if lower-income residents of color are in control of land, then the CLT can support the mobilization and empowerment of those residents and the broader community to demand land and resources from public and private entities and enable equitable development to fulfill the needs of residents of color. The result can be mixed-income, racially inclusive communities that not only survive through market pressures but thrive through diverse interconnectedness.

CLTS REALIZING A RECONCILED APPROACH: THREE EXAMPLES

The three cases that follow profile CLTs developed at different points in time by diverse actors that have, or are working to adopt, approaches that concurrently prioritize community control and scaling up. Dudley Neighbors is the story of a *grassroots organizing effort* that created a CLT subsidiary to pursue land acquisition with community control, recognizing that residents needed to garner power and control over the fate of their neighborhood. City of Lakes Community Land Trust is the story of a *coalition* that formed and decided a city-wide CLT was needed, leading to the mobilization of communities across neighborhoods and, ultimately, formation of a new community around the CLT's mission and governance. In this example, a network of CLTs across the state, along with residents and community stakeholders, effectively foster resources. Houston Community Land Trust is the story of a *local government* that is bringing political will, land, and major financial resources to the table, ushering forward the CLT idea brought forward by community groups as a needed tool. It holds promise to be the fastest- growing CLT that develops community control across neighborhoods.

These cases illustrate how CLTs can use various reconciled approaches to advance both community control and the growth of land in trust. They also support that balancing these two priorities must be an ongoing, intentional endeavor.

Dudley Neighbors, Inc. and Dudley Street Neighborhood Initiative

Like so many other inner-city neighborhoods across the country, the Dudley and Roxbury neighborhood in the city of Boston experienced extreme disinvestment in the 1970s and early 1980s. What was once an almost entirely white neighborhood in 1950 experienced white flight to such an extreme that only 14 percent of the population remained white by 1990, and the neighborhood lost roughly 40 percent of its total population. The poverty and unemployment rates for residents was almost double that of Boston. Real estate development stopped in the neighborhood, while slumlords and speculative land owners moved in to make money from operating unsafe, substandard housing and holding land. Meanwhile, waste removal companies and private companies illegally used vacant parcels as their dumping grounds.

By the mid-1980s, residents had had enough.[14] In 1984 they formed the Dudley Street Neighborhood Initiative (DSNI), a community-based planning and organizing nonprofit, to reclaim their neighborhood. DSNI's mission is "to empower Dudley residents to organize, plan for, create and control a vibrant, diverse and high-quality neighborhood in collaboration with community partners."[15] Within the decade, Dudley residents had completed a comprehensive planning process to address the 1,300 parcels of abandoned land in the neighborhood. The City of Boston adopted their comprehensive plan, which included the creation of a community land trust called Dudley Neighbors, Inc. (DNI).

In an historic act of relinquishing control to an organized community, the City granted DNI the power of eminent domain for abandoned properties within the 62 acres of the Dudley Triangle. The community land trust hired staff, including neighborhood residents and people with experience in financing and development, and they began implementing the community's plan. Today, DNI holds more than 30 acres of formerly vacant and abandoned land in trust. This land now includes 227 affordable homes and over 10 more in the development pipeline—some shared equity and some rentals—as well as commercial space, a commercial greenhouse, urban farm, gardens, parks, and playgrounds.

Neighborhood residents continue to control development activities in the Dudley neighborhood through the formal review and approval of all new projects and by the neighborhood initiative's governance structure. Thirty-two of the seats on the Dudley Street Neighborhood Initiative's 34-member board are up for election every two years, and neighborhood residents are educated on the elections and candidates before casting their ballots. Sixteen board seats are for representatives of the racial and ethnic groups that reside in Dudley, including Blacks (4), Latinos (4), Cape Verdeans (4), and Caucasians (4), and three board seats are for youth representatives. The community land trust's board is composed of nine members, of which two non-voting seats are held by state legislators. In order to prevent election fatigue, six of the nine voting members are appointed by the DSNI board, and four of those board members live or work on the land in trust. The remaining seats are appointments by the Neighborhood Council, city council member, and mayor.

Dudley Neighbors, Inc., was established to "realize a vision of development without displacement."[16] DSNI leaders established the community land trust as a separate nonprofit subsidiary because they expected that, as the community organizing entity, DSNI would dissolve after resident leadership was cultivated, community planning was completed, and the land was acquired. They also wanted to ensure that the practical constraints of development being handled by DNI were addressed separately from the broad-based community visioning and planning process organized by DSNI. Ultimately, community members decided to continue with both entities as complimentary anchor institutions so that DSNI could foster youth and resident leadership development, raise funds, and facilitate training, organizing, and community-requested programs while DNI continued acquiring land, overseeing development, and stewarding a growing portfolio on behalf of the community.

DSNI/DNI is an example of a community land trust that has kept resident control of land at the forefront without sacrificing scale in its land holdings. In fact, scaling the trust's portfolio to enact residents' vision was a primary driver of community organizing.

When the long-standing Boston Mayor Tom Menino left office in 2014, DSNI and DNI advocated to ensure that eminent domain and political will for the community land trust remained intact during changes in city leadership and staff. Impressively, during the start of Mayor Martin J. Walsh's first term, John Barros—a Dudley resident, former youth leader, and current executive director of DSNI— became the city's chief of economic development.

Once deemed "undesirable" and "blighted," the Dudley neighborhood now faces encroaching pressure from private development. Luckily, through the land trust the community continues to have the right to claim vacant land, and community control continues to grow larger and stronger. Dudley is now a mixed-income, racially diverse community that practices neighborly engagement and collective advocacy to attract resources, influence private real estate developers, maintain political will, and position long-time residents as the leaders and beneficiaries of community change. Because the community land trust ensures that there will always be homes for lower-income house-holds, the neighborhood should remain economically and racially integrated.

City of Lakes Community Land Trust

In many ways, Minneapolis is the quintessential midwestern city. In the 1950s, new high-ways and inexpensive mortgages lured the mostly white middle class to the suburbs. As that trend continued into the 1980s, the city's population fell. During the same period, the Twin Cities' racial diversity increased, as churches sponsored refugees and immi-grants from Cambodia, Laos, and Vietnam in the 1970s; the former Soviet Union in the 1980s; and Somalia, Ethiopia, and Liberia in the 1990s. The people who remained in Minneapolis as the suburbs grew included a larger proportion of people of color, both because of diversification overall and due to redlining in the suburbs. Minneapolis' pop-ulation began to grow again in the 1990s. The city's population is now double the 1950 total and approximately 60 percent white.[17]

As the Minneapolis housing market began to heat up in 2001, driven by the growth in population and the large proportion of households needing affordable housing, a coali-tion formed in South Minneapolis. Members included the Powderhorn Residents Group, Seward Redesign, Powderhorn Park Neighborhood Association, and the Lyndale Neigh-borhood Development Corporation. Through research and community meetings, coa-lition members realized that the entire city could benefit from a community land trust. They incorporated the City of Lakes Community Land Trust (CLCLT) in fall 2002.[18]

As a city-wide rather than neighborhood-based community land trust, CLCLT took a different approach to engaging residents and fostering community control. CLT staff conducted intensive education and outreach to neighborhood associations and commu-nity groups, presenting the land trust as an asset or tool residents could use if they felt pressure from outside development. As Executive Director Jeff Washburne said in a 2007 interview:

We've gone out and met with all of the Minneapolis neighborhood organizations. We went to their meetings and talked about the land trust, but didn't ask them to provide us with anything. We wanted them to see us as a community asset, but one that doesn't require any neighborhood resources. The only thing we asked of them was to think about the CLT model, particularly if there was potential for a housing development to be built in their neighborhood. Our message was, "If you and your neighbors feel that the development requires affordability—especially long-term affordability—then your neighborhood association should suggest that the developer come and talk to us." In more than one instance, neighborhood groups have told developers to talk to us before the groups would agree to move forward on a project.[19]

City of Lakes CLT has a 15-person board composed of one-third lessees and one-third community members. Approximately 350 community members across Minneapolis, along with the residents living on land in trust, form the corporate community membership.[20] By the end of 2018, the CLCLT had 272 homeownership units and four rental units maintained as permanently affordable in the trust and was on track to have about 40 more homes for sale. The proportion of CLCLT homeowners who are persons of color has reached 53 percent, relative to only 24 percent of all homeowners in Minneapolis.[21] CLCLT leaders hope to acquire more land and create as many permanently affordable homes as possible before Minneapolis becomes a runaway market like some other cities, rendering it prohibitively expensive to create mixed-income communities. They plan to rehabilitate or construct homes in neighborhoods that have not experienced major "warming" yet as well as working in areas that have already gentrified. The latter is harder because it costs more, but the CLT is strategically tracking tax foreclosure sales and has a program that allows prospective homeowners to find homes in the market and bring them into the CLT.

As the CLT's portfolio and number of residents increased and their relationships in the broader community have grown, a community of residents, stakeholders, and supporters formed around the CLT and helped drive its success. Residents have testified in public, at budget hearings, and to their city council to ensure that resources are maintained for affordable housing and directed to shared equity homeownership. Residents and community members show up when mobilized by the CLT for advocacy, and they open their homes and share their stories with policymakers and prospective funders of the CLT. As importantly, City of Lakes CLT joins with other CLTs across the state to promote partnerships and resources through their state housing finance agency, Minnesota Housing, which provides subsidies to CLTs through competitive grantmaking and mortgages for CLT homebuyers.

Now community members are calling upon the CLT for two new endeavors. One involves acquiring or creating commercial developments to be held in trust. Pressure is mounting on Minneapolis' light-rail corridors and nodes, so council members and their constituents are asking the CLT to secure land for businesses needed by the community or to help preserve commercial spaces so that small-business owners are not displaced. The hope is that the CLT can stem the tides of both economic and cultural displacement, but it has yet to be seen if the City will come up with needed financial resources for this endeavor. Second, tenant advocacy groups have asked the CLT to explore the creation and preservation of limited equity cooperatives (LECs) on land held in trust. This will not only prevent displacement of existing residents but also ensure that the land is forever dedicated to affordable housing, while the buildings will be directly governed by the LEC residents.

CLT Director Washburne sees the community requests as evidence of success. "When we started this work, racial equity and displacement were not being talked about, so we couldn't really lead with that kind of message," he observes. "Sixteen years later, we lead with the importance of community control of land for racial justice and mixed-income communities. I think we're at a turning point where we have clout with funders and can work the systems for community control. So, we want more grassroots groups telling us where to go and what to do. We want them to drive, and we'll be the horsepower."[22]

City of Houston and the Houston Community Land Trust

As community land trusts have gained attention as a tool to buffer gentrification while providing stable, permanently affordable homeownership and rental opportunities, a growing number of municipalities are taking the lead in launching CLTs. One such place is Houston, Texas. Nonprofit organizations and neighborhood groups, such as Row House Community Development Corporation and Emancipation Economic Development Council, began exploring the CLT concept in 2015 as a way to address mounting concerns over realized and anticipated increases in housing values and gentrification in predominantly Black neighborhoods. Residents of Third Ward, for instance, saw housing values climb 176% from 2000 to 2013; more recently, high-end development came with a $34 million redevelopment of Emancipation Park.[23] Listening to residents and community leaders, the City worked with Grounded Solutions Network to begin exploration and planning for a community land trust.[24]

And then on August 24, 2017, Hurricane Harvey hit, and the City moved into crisis mode. Well over a year later, Houston—along with the other areas affected in Texas—was still waiting to receive $5 billion in Community Development Block Grant-Disaster Recovery (CDBG-DR) funds. As noted in *The New York Times,* communities of color were disproportionally affected and hurting from the storm's impact; as Mayor Sylvester Turner stated, "There are thousands of families who live in low-income communities who already were operating at the margins before Harvey, and the storm pushed them down even further."[25]

Despite the disaster, the City resumed working with Grounded Solutions Network in 2018 to develop a community land trust. The Housing and Community Development Department realized that the CLT might be a critical tool during rebuilding to serve lower-income families and communities of color who were displaced or had their neighborhoods destroyed by the storm, and to help bring racial equity and economic integration to rebuild Houston neighborhoods. They worked to align other local resources, policies, and tools with the future CLT. This effort included using the Houston Land Bank to usher properties over to the community land trust and planning to bring multimillion-dollar funding to CLT development through Tax Increment Reinvestment Zones. After working with Grounded Solutions and other consultants to build out the framework and business model, the City then created a new nonprofit organization, the Houston Community Land Trust.

City leaders realized that the CLT could not be a governmental entity; rather, it had to be an independently governed nonprofit and advocate on behalf of the communities where it works to ensure the CLT is sustainable beyond political changes. In partnership with community stakeholders, City staff held community events to inform and gathered input from community members and stakeholders. Over the course of a year, the board of directors was recruited, the first two staff were hired, and the CLT broke ground on its first three homes. Leaders expect to add over 50 homes by the end of 2019 while staff and board members continue to convene public education events, conduct outreach to resident groups, and build relationships with leaders in the neighborhoods where the CLT will work.

The Houston CLT is positioned to be the fastest-growing CLT in the nation due to the enabling policies, resources, and City support. However, the CLT will have a daunting task of building resident leadership and community control as it grows and works in different neighborhoods across Houston. Similar to City of Lakes CLT, the intent is to partner with community organizations and neighborhood groups, offering a tool that communities can deploy to build high-quality, affordable housing that will last in disinvested or disaster-hit areas and in areas facing gentrification and displacement pressures. Over time, the CLT plans to create a corporate community membership and adopt a new board structure (once they have residents), ensuring resident leadership and representation from the various neighborhoods where they hold land in trust. The CLT also plans to organize and mobilize communities to ensure that the resources and political will for community control of land in trust creates a mixed-income, racially integrated Houston that lasts long into the future.

LESSONS LEARNED

Whether they are building homes in recovering, revitalizing, gentrifying, or high-opportunity areas, all of the CLTs profiled here have created or are fostering the creation and preservation of mixed-income, racially inclusive communities in which households not only have a place but also a say over the fate of their neighborhood(s). What can we learn from these examples about using a reconciled approach?

Community Engagement and Control Will Manifest Differently Due to Varying Context

Because of the differences in how each CLT was established, "community" is defined differently and, therefore, "community control" is manifested differently—at least in part—in each example. Part of the difference lies in how residents and other members of the community interact with the CLT. For Dudley Neighborhood Initiative, residents of the neighborhood (lessees and non-lessees of the CLT) are literally walking by or on the land held in trust every day. They are organized by the parent nonprofit, DSNI, to direct land disposition strategies, and residents of CLT properties have meaningful board representation. For City of Lakes, residents of CLT properties have formed a new community around the organization, representing various neighborhoods where they live in the CLT's membership, governance, and advocacy. Place-based communities call upon City of Lakes CLT to influence neighborhood development and, if they are members, approve of CLT developments. For Houston, the nonprofit CLT has just been born, so there are no residents on land held in trust yet. But community members are being informed and engaged so the CLT can form a board with resident representation and neighborhood groups can influence the CLT's development. In time, all three CLTs arguably will have meaningful community engagement and accountability to residents on land held in trust and in the broader community.

Regardless of Context, Larger Land Holdings Translate to Increased Community Control

Focusing solely on governance and authority misses a critical component of "community control" that comes to light if we answer, "How much of the community *geographically* do community members and residents control?" Under the mission and obligations of a CLT, meaningful land holdings allot residents and community members more power. For instance, DSNI and DNI serve a small geography, but they are a force to be reckoned with for private development efforts that attempt to come into their neighborhood. City of Lakes CLT does not have the same levels of local political and financial support, and it could be due to their larger service area even though they have a slightly larger and faster-growing portfolio than DNI. Meanwhile, if the Houston CLT grows at the clip expected, the CLT's residents and community membership have the potential to organize and influence private development as well as local policy and resources (if the political will fades in the future). Larger land holdings mean that the community controls more—both in terms of community development and political capital.

Community Organizing Groups and CLTs Should Maximize Their Distinctive Roles

A lesson learned from both DSNI and DNI as separate entities—and City of Lakes CLT now partnering with tenant advocacy groups—is that community organizing and the

CLT are effective complements. Remember, CLTs are nonprofits that have made a *permanent* commitment to stewarding land for the community, so they must be perceived as reliable, productive, and effective to policymakers and funders. Grassroots community groups can do more confrontational organizing, running short-term campaigns that use direct tactics to apply political pressure for funding and policies. Consequently, grassroots community organizing groups are more often going to be better off if they remain the steadfast advocates for a CLT rather than trying to become a nonprofit CLT doing development. We believe grassroots groups will get further in their goals if they find a nonprofit partner with the capacity to house the CLT and steward the land under community control.

CLTs and Their Stakeholders Should Adopt "Inside-Outside" Advocacy Strategies for Enabling Policies and Obtaining Revenue

Unfortunately, efforts to build enabling policies and obtain dedicated revenue for CLTs are not happening across many of the localities that would benefit from CLTs. In their absence, scale remains modest (even in the case studies). Using a reconciled approach, CLTs should adopt an "inside-outside" advocacy strategy whereby residents, community members, and advocates organize campaigns for policies and funding from outside of government, while the staff and board of the CLT lead or participate in coalitions to set strategic policy goals, coordinate stakeholders, and partner with policymakers inside government. Organized communities can push policymakers and government leaders to prioritize resources for the CLT (and to require permanent affordability when resources are deployed) and to pass enabling legislation for equitable land use and mixed-income, racially inclusive community development. Hence, CLTs should celebrate—even cultivate—the role of residents and community members as mobilizers, organizers, and advocates. Ultimately, CLTs will not proliferate if they are simply competing against other affordable housing nonprofits for scarce existing resources. Instead, they need to mobilize communities to build an infrastructure that reliably produces land in trust and a greater number of permanently affordable homes.

IMPLICATIONS FOR ACTION

Adopting a reconciled approach that values both community control and meaningful land in trust will maximize creating or maintaining mixed-income, racially inclusive communities by CLTs. We call upon the field to never forget that land is power and people united is power. Below are recommendations for how to advance both.

Implications for Policy

- As CLTs are developing or pursuing sustainability, dedicated funding sources and enabling policies should be developed in tandem, which requires educating policymakers and elected officials on CLTs. This may include establishing local sources and policies (see below), as well as prioritizing permanent affordability for competitive federal funding programs, such as HOME or the Community Development Block Grant Program.

- CLTs and their stakeholders need to analyze which enabling policies and funding sources are most practical in their local and state political contexts. For instance, in places with local housing trust funds, the CLT and its stakeholders could work to ensure that the fund requires or prioritizes lasting affordability. For places using tax increment financing, CLTs and stakeholders should advocate for ensuring that a portion of homes created with tax increment financing funds are permanently affordable and stewarded by the CLT. CLTs and stakeholders also should advocate for new and existing land banks to provide a pipeline of discounted or donated land. Lastly, CLTs and advocates should promote inclusionary housing policies that require affordable homes to be placed in trust.

Implications for Research and Evaluation

- Research on variations in organizational structures, governance structures, community memberships, and resident and community leadership and engagement activities should examine the impact on "community control" and growth.

- Further research on housing in CLTs should examine whether it buffers the adverse effects of gentrification as well as creates and maintains mixed-income, racially inclusive communities.

- Researchers should assess the economic feasibility of a rent-to-shared equity homeownership fund. The field must pursue innovative financing strategies that minimize the reliance on subsidies to expand the affordable housing produced by CLTs. Although in its nascent conceptual stage, Grounded Solutions Network hopes to explore the feasibility of a fund that would pursue single-family acquisitions in relatively low-cost markets that are on the cusp of gentrification and facing displacement pressures. The homes would be rehabbed and rented to families with a local CLT as the responsible "landlord." In three to 10 years, when the value of homes in the private market has appreciated, the rented homes would be converted into shared equity homes held by the CLT. After debt is repaid in the conversion, the appreciation effectively provides the subsidy to cover the difference between the market-rate value of the home and the discounted purchase price that a lower-income family can afford. If a fund like this proves feasible, it could substantially generate homes on land in trust that are community controlled and result in mixed-income, racially inclusive neighborhoods.

Implications for Development and Investment

■ CLTs need to prioritize community participation and leadership—especially amongst Black and Brown stakeholders—in the disposition strategies for land in trust, and they must partner with grassroots groups to garner the necessary resources for the community's development vision to come to fruition.

■ CLTs also need to maintain partnerships and collaboration with government offices, political officials, funders, and financial institutions for their ongoing sustainability.

■ The field needs to shift from reliance on public funds to program-related investments and private financing by creating unique fund structures to advance scale, such as (1) acquisition funds and (2) single-family rent-to-shared equity homeownership funds (see above).

Implications for Residents and Community Members

■ Residents and community members of the CLT—especially people of color— should join the corporate community membership, assume leadership positions, and engage in land disposition decisions whenever possible.

■ Residents and community members should advocate for the CLT to build political will, secure financial resources, and pass enabling policies that will increase community-controlled land and developments.

Notes

This essay was previously published in *What Works to Promote Inclusive, Equitable Mixed-Income Communities,* Mark L. Joseph and Amy T. Khare, Eds., 2020, National Initiative on Mixed-Income Communities at the Jack, Joseph, and Morton Mandel School of Applied Social Sciences, Case Western Reserve University, as part of the What Works Series of the Federal Reserve Bank of San Francisco. Minor changes have been made to the original essay.

1. Robert J. Chaskin and Mark L. Joseph, *Integrating the Inner City: The Promise and Perils of Mixed-Income Public Housing Transformation* (Chicago: University of Chicago Press, 2015).

2. Nicholas Shatan and Olivia Williams, *A Guide to Transformative Land Strategies: Lessons from the Field* (Cambridge, MA: Massachusetts Institute of Technology's Community Innovators Lab, June 2015), p. 3.

3. There are many "colder" urban neighborhoods where this pattern does not take place, and revitalization stalls without attracting private investment.

4. Federal housing programs require that rehabbed or newly constructed housing must remain affordable anywhere from 5–30 years, which are insufficient periods to retain the affordable housing stock over the long-term.

5. Dan Immergluck, personal communication, February 28, 2019.

6. Carolina Katz Reid, "Achieving the American dream? A longitudinal analysis of the homeownership experiences of low-income households," (CSD Working Paper 05–20, Center for Social Development, Washington University, St. Louis, MO, 2005).

7. Emily Thaden, "Stable Home Ownership in a Turbulent Economy: Delinquencies and Foreclosures Remain Low in Community Land Trusts," (Working Paper WP412ET1, Lincoln Institute of Land Policy, Cambridge, MA, 2011).

8. Myungshik Choi, Shannon Van Zandt, and David Matarrita-Cascante, "Can community land trusts slow gentrification?," *Journal of Urban Affairs* 40, no. 3 (2018): 394–411.

9. Choi et al., "Can community land trusts slow gentrification?," 394–411.

10. Ruoniu Wang, Claire Cahen, Arthur Acolin, Rebecca J. Walter. "Tracking Growth and Evaluating Performance of Shared Equity Homeownership Programs During Housing Market Fluctuations," (Working Paper WP19RW1, Lincoln Institute of Land Policy, Cambridge, MA, 2019).

11. https://www.arcofjusticefilm.com/

12. https://snccdigital.org/events/new-communities-formed-in-southwest-georgia/

13. Nicholas Shatan and Olivia Williams, *A Guide to Transformative Land Strategies: Lessons from the Field* (Cambridge, MA: Massachusetts Institute of Technology's Community Innovators Lab, June 2015), p. 43–44.

14. Peter Medoff and Holly Sklar, *Streets of Hope: The Rise and Fall of an Urban Neighborhood.* (Cambridge, MA: South End Press, 1994); and Holding Ground: The Rebirth of Dudley Street, directed by Leah Mahan and Mark Lipman, (1996; Boston, MA: Holding Ground Productions).

15. Dudley Street Neighborhood Initiative, accessed August 26, 2019, https://www.dsni.org/.

16. Dudley Neighbors, Inc., accessed August 26, 2019, https://www.dudleyneighbors.org/.

17. Greta Kaul, "Minneapolis is growing at its fastest rate since 1950," *MinnPost,* May 23, 2018, https://www.minnpost.com/politics-policy/2018/05/minneapolis-growing -its-fastest-rate-1950/. Minnesota State Demographic Center, "Minnesota Now, Then, When . . . An Overview of Demographic Change," August 28, 2019, https://mn.gov/ admin/assets/2015-04-06-overview-MN-demographic-changes_tcm36-74549.pdf.

18. City of Lakes Community Land Trust, accessed August 28, 2019, http://www.clclt.org/.

19. Federal Reserve Bank of Minneapolis, "A conversation with Jeff Washburne—Director, City of Lakes Community Land Trust," accessed on August 28, 2019. https://www. minneapolisfed.org/publications/community- dividend/a-conversation-with-jeff-washburne-director-city-of-lakes-community-land-trust?sc_device=Default.

20. City of Lakes Community Land Trust, "2018 Annual Report," accessed on August 28, 2019, http://www.clclt.org/wp-content/uploads/2019/01/Final-Annual-Report _10232018.pdf.

21. Federal Reserve Bank of Minneapolis, "A conversation with Jeff Washburne," 2019.

22. Federal Reserve Bank of Minneapolis, "A conversation with Jeff Washburne," 2019.

23. Leah Binkovitz, "In Houston, A Radical Approach to Affordable Housing," *Urban Edge Blog,* June 6, 2018, https://kinder.rice.edu/2018/06/06/houston-radical-approach -affordable-housing.

24. Grounded Solutions Network, "Community Land Trust Business Plan," accessed on August 28, 2019, https://www.houstontx.gov/council/committees/housing/20170201 /community-land-trust.pdf.

25. Manny Fernandez, "A Year After Hurricane Harvey, Houston's Poorest Neighborhoods Are Slowest to Recover," *The New York Times,* September 3, 2018. https://www.nytimes. com/2018/09/03/us/hurricane-harvey-houston.html.

References

Binkovitz, Leah. "In Houston, A Radical Approach to Affordable Housing." *Urban Edge Blog,* June 6, 2018. https://kinder.rice.edu/2018/06/06/houston-radical-approach-affordable-housing.

Chaskin, Robert J. and Mark L. Joseph. *Integrating the Inner City: The Promise and Perils of Mixed-Income Public Housing Transformation.* Chicago: University of Chicago Press, 2015.

Choi, Myungshik, Shannon Van Zandt, and David Matarrita-Cascante. "Can community land trusts slow gentrification?." *Journal of Urban Affairs* 40, no. 3 (2018): 394–411.

City of Lakes Community Land Trust. Accessed August 28, 2019. http://www.clclt.org/.

City of Lakes Community Land Trust. "2018 Annual Report." Accessed on August 28, 2019. http://www.clclt.org/wp-content/uploads/2019/01/Final-Annual-Report_10232018. pdf.

Dudley Neighbors, Inc. Accessed August 26, 2019. https://www.dudleyneighbors.org/.

Dudley Street Neighborhood Initiative. Accessed August 26, 2019. https://www.dsni.org/.

Federal Reserve Bank of Minneapolis. "A conversation with Jeff Washburne—Director, City of Lakes Community Land Trust." Accessed on August 28, 2019. https://www. minneapolisfed.org/publications/community-dividend/a-conversation-with-jeff-washburne-director-city-of-lakes-community-land-trust?sc_device=Default.

Fernandez, Manny. "A Year After Hurricane Harvey, Houston's Poorest Neighborhoods Are Slowest to Recover." *The New York Times,* September 3, 2018. https://www. nytimes.com/2018/09/03/us/hurricane-harvey-houston.html.

Grounded Solutions Network. "Community Land Trust Business Plan." Accessed on August 28, 2019. https://www.houstontx.gov/council/committees/housing/20170201/community-land-trust.pdf.

Kaul, Greta. "Minneapolis is growing at its fastest rate since 1950." *MinnPost,* May 23, 2018. https://www.minnpost.com/politics-policy/2018/05/minneapolis-growing-its-fastest-rate-1950/.

Mahan, Leah and Mark Lipman, dir. *Holding Ground: The Rebirth of Dudley Street.* 1996; Boston, MA: Holding Ground Productions.

Medoff, Peter and Holly Sklar. *Streets of Hope: The Rise and Fall of an Urban Neighborhood.* Cambridge, MA: South End Press, 1994.

Minnesota State Demographic Center. "Minnesota Now, Then, When... An Overview of Demographic Change." Accessed August 28, 2019.

https://mn.gov/admin/assets/2015-04-06-overview-MN-demographic-changes_tcm36-74549.pdf.

Reid, Carolina Katz. "Achieving the American dream? A longitudinal analysis of the home-ownership experiences of low-income households." CSD Working Paper 05-20, Center for Social Development, Washington University, St. Louis, MO, 2005.

Shatan, Nicholas and Olivia Williams. *A Guide to Transformative Land Strategies: Lessons from the Field.* Cambridge, MA: Massachusetts Institute of Technology's Community Innovators Lab, June 2015.

Thaden, Emily. "Stable Home Ownership in a Turbulent Economy: Delinquencies and Foreclosures Remain Low in Community Land Trusts." Working Paper WP412ET1, Lincoln Institute of Land Policy, Cambridge, MA, 2011.

Wang, Ruoniu, Claire Cahen, Arthur Acolin, and Rebecca J. Walter. "Tracking Growth and Evaluating Performance of Shared Equity Homeownership Programs During Housing Market Fluctuations." Working Paper WP19RW1, Lincoln Institute of Land Policy, Cambridge, MA, 2019.

2.

The Best Things in Life
Are Perpetually Affordable
Profile of the Champlain Housing Trust, Burlington, Vermont

Brenda M. Torpy

The Champlain Housing Trust (CHT) was born in a small city with a big idea: by creating a stock of permanently affordable housing, everyone could have access to a decent, affordable home, regardless of income. This was the grand vision of a newly elected progressive government led by Mayor Bernie Sanders who came into office in 1981, the same year as Ronald Reagan became President of the United States.

The so-called Reagan Revolution resulted in massive reductions in federal funding for affordable housing and forced the Sanders administration to develop innovative solutions to address Burlington's housing problems. Equally challenging were double-digit mortgage rates that prevailed during the 1980s, the threatened gentrification of Burlington's traditional working class neighborhoods, and the long-standing neglect of housing quality and affordability by previous mayors. They had favored downtown commercial development and had allowed low-income neighborhoods to be bulldozed in the name of Urban Renewal.

A cornerstone of the progressive agenda was to open up City Hall to all citizens — especially those who had been previously excluded — involving them in decisions about city planning and public funding. One of Bernie's earliest allies on the City Council, Terry Bouricius, had heard about community land trusts and suggested it might be a good fit for Burlington. The model's democratic structure and its commitment to permanent affordability made a lot of sense in a city where housing costs were on the rise, where a lack of code enforcement and the absence of landlord-tenant law made low-income tenants nearly powerless in the overheated housing market, and where proposed waterfront development adjacent to the city's lowest-income area, the Old North End, threatened further gentrification.

When Mayor Sanders created the Community and Economic Development Office (CEDO) in 1983 to help implement his progressive agenda, work on establishing a community land trust soon got underway. CEDO sent several employees to the first national CLT gathering in Voluntown Connecticut, hosted by the Institute for Community Economics (ICE). Included in this CEDO delegation were Michael Monte, the City's community development director, and Brenda Torpy, the City's housing director. At the Voluntown conference, they met John Davis who was a technical assistance provider on ICE's staff. A few months later, CEDO contracted with ICE to bring Davis to Burlington to introduce the CLT idea to Burlington's citizens and to see if it would take root.

> The Burlington Community Land Trust was the first municipally initiated and municipally supported CLT in the United States.

It did. The Burlington Community Land Trust (BCLT) was incorporated in 1984 after thousands of hours of volunteer work. Recruited and coordinated by CEDO staff, these volunteers wrote bylaws for the new organization, developed its policies, and fashioned strategies for finding the funds that would be needed to support the organization's operations and to produce affordable housing. Among the BCLT's incorporators were Howard Dean, the state's future Governor, and Sarah Carpenter, future director of the Vermont Housing Finance Agency. The Old North End was chosen as the BCLT's area of priority, although the BCLT's bylaws allowed the organization to look for housing development opportunities in any of Burlington's neighborhoods.

The City government seeded the fledging CLT effort with a $200,000 grant for operations and provided a pair of million-dollar loans from the Burlington Employees' Retirement System. The BCLT later received regular municipal funding for its operations and its projects through federal funds that passed through the City's hands, including monies provided by the federal Community Development Block Grant and HOME programs, and from local funds disbursed by Burlington's Housing Trust Fund. Beyond financial support, the BCLT also had the benefit of continued assistance from CEDO staff and from Davis, the ICE staffer assigned to Burlington under a CEDO contract.

The Burlington Community Land Trust was the first municipally initiated and municipally supported CLT in the United States, a direct result of the City's embrace of permanent affordability, a policy deemed by Progressives in City Hall to be the only socially equitable and fiscally prudent way for the public to create and to sustain affordable housing. Mayor Bernie Sanders and his immediate successor, Peter Clavelle, were outspoken champions of "decommodifying" publicly assisted, privately owned housing. Their administrations acted to embed this principle into municipal policy and multiple ordinances. Their goal was to ensure that public investments in affordable housing would go primarily — even exclusively — into housing that would be kept *permanently* affordable. This was viewed as a revolutionary idea at the time, an outgrowth of Bernie's socialist agenda. But over the years, and for very practical reasons, this commitment to permanent affordability became accepted wisdom throughout Vermont. It also slowly gained acceptance among city officials in many other states.

SEEDING INNOVATION OUTSIDE OF CITY HALL

It came as a surprise to many of Bernie's political opponents — and to some of his supporters — that a majority of the most progressive measures enacted by this self-described socialist were delegated to *non*governmental organizations, either to private, nonprofit organizations that had been around for many years or to nonprofits that were newly created. These progressive measures may have been initiated by City Hall, but they were neither administered nor controlled by city government. That was true for the BCLT as well.

What was the thinking of the Sanders Administration in choosing to establish the Burlington Community Land Trust as an autonomous entity *outside* of city government, one that was guided and governed by private citizens? The reasons behind this decision were both practical and political, a multi-faceted rationale that unfolded as follows.

First, nonprofit, non-governmental organizations (NGOs) in the United States have access to sources of project funding and operational support that governmental organizations do not. NGOs like the Burlington Community Land Trust can receive an exemption from federal income taxes, a status known as a 501(c)(3) designation. This status helps nonprofit organizations to raise donations from private citizens, since donors may deduct such gifts from their own federal taxes. Today, the

Fig. 2.1. Bernie Sanders, speaking at the National CLT Conference, Burlington, Vermont, 1990.

Champlain Housing Trust raises $200,000 a year in this way, and has also built to date a capital endowment of $2,000,000 from private donations. CHT uses a portion of the annual earnings from this endowment to help fund its operations, keeping the principle intact while collecting about $100,000 a year in revenue. This "rainy day fund" has enabled CHT to be a bolder and more innovative developer. CLT's 501(c)(3) status also allows the organization to apply for funding from corporate and private philanthropic foundations, as well as from government programs that often require applicants to have a tax exemption as a condition of eligibility.

Second, the BCLT was established outside of the municipal government because city administrations come and go. Policies, programs, and priorities can change dramatically with every change in government. In Burlington, the Progressives never dreamed they would control City Hall throughout the 1980s and for much of the 1990s. They hoped to perpetuate progressive policies like permanent affordability, therefore, by institutionalizing them outside of city government.

The BCLT adopted the "classic" CLT model of a broad-based membership and a representative board because it met the Sanders administration's commitment to a more democratic approach to community development. From the outset, the BCLT's leadership consciously used this structure to expand the constituency for its mission by recruiting leadership from beyond the Progressive circle and found that, when separated from the heat of Burlington's partisan politics, the BCLT's mission found wide support. Even some conservative politicians came to embrace permanent affordability, recognizing it to be a more efficient use of public funds.[1] The BCLT's leadership was also well aware that the whole idea of a community land trust was pushing against the conventions of the private real estate market and the powerful interests that undergird it. A community-based NGO that embraced advocacy and education as part of its core mission could mobilize its members to support and defend progressive projects and policies as needed.

For example, in 1993 the citizens of Burlington elected a Republican mayor, Peter Brownell, after a decade of Progressive rule. The new mayor soon proposed to redirect community development funding away from affordable housing in order to support economic development and public works instead. The BCLT led the resistance to his efforts. When City Councilors met to take the vote on the mayor's proposal, they found themselves surrounded by seventeen quilted banners hanging from the upper balcony of the council chamber. Each colorful banner, three feet wide and eight feet in length, was made up of dozens of hand-sewn squares. These quilt squares, 500 in all, had been crafted by residents of affordable housing and homeless shelters throughout Burlington, who had been asked to depict the meaning of home in images and words of their own choosing. One square, in particular, captured the BCLT's unique approach to housing: "The Best Things in Life Are Perpetually Affordable." As the City Council's meeting got underway, volunteers stepped to the microphone during the public forum, reading statements that spoke of the importance of affordable housing in their own lives. In the end, the Council voted to restore the housing funds, rejecting Mayor Brownell's proposal. The Mayor himself lasted for only a single, two-year term. He lost the next election and Progressives returned to power.

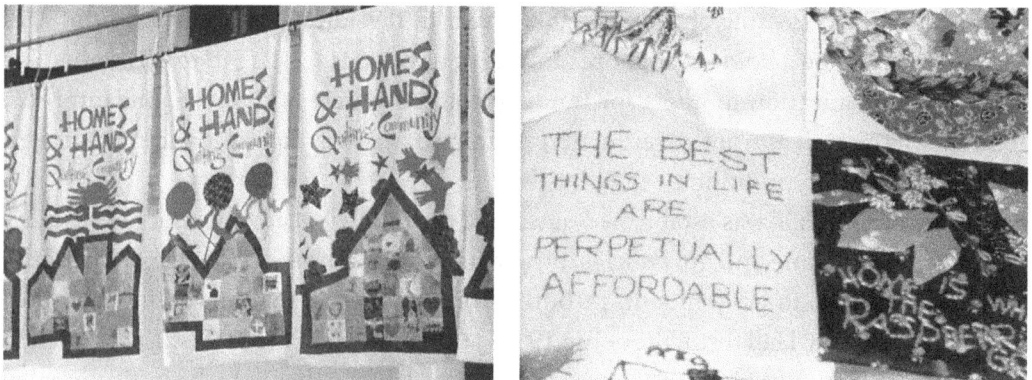

Fig 2.2. Quilted banners hanging in Burlington City Hall, 1993 (left). Detail of quilt squares (right).

Another reason for establishing the BCLT outside of city government was the sheer unfamiliarity of the whole idea of developing and selling resale-restricted, owner-occupied homes on leased land. It was easier to market such homes if the landowner was a charitable, nonprofit organization rather than a governmental entity. It was easier for the public to accept the overall concept as well. If the Sanders administration had attempted to institute *government* ownership of land, it would have fed into the Red-baiting narrative of Bernie's opponents. Vermont was and still is a very liberal part of the United States, but property rights are jealously guarded and government interference in these rights through any type of property restriction has always created a strong backlash.

There was a final, practical reason for creating a community land trust outside of city government, one that became increasingly clear in subsequent years. The BCLT was going to be a better steward for a growing portfolio of permanently affordable, owner-occupied homes than city officials could ever be. Long-term stewardship required a specialized staff who were fully committed to watching over the housing entrusted into their care, acting to protect the housing's affordability and intervening, when necessary, to prevent foreclosures among any homeowners who might get behind in their mortgage payments.[2] Stewardship, in order to work easily and effectively, would require a cooperative relationship between the land trust and its homeowners, who are also members of the CLT. This is not the kind of relationship that can be easily created or maintained with a government agency.

CULTIVATING A FAVORABLE POLICY ENVIRONMENT

As Burlington's Progressives worked to create new resources for the development of affordable housing, they also worked to enact new laws that would protect vulnerable renters and produce permanently affordable homes through funding and policy initiatives. This dual commitment to expanding the supply of housing and to preserving the affordability of that housing was woven into guidelines for the Housing Trust Fund, capitalized through a penny increase on the property tax rate; ordinances that regulated the conversion of rental housing to condominiums and retarded the loss of existing housing from demolition or conversion to commercial uses; and an Inclusionary Zoning (IZ) ordinance, where the affordability of all IZ units had to be preserved for 99 years.[3]

Creating these laws required the active participation of many of the same neighborhood activists and housing advocates who had come together to create the BCLT in 1984. The board and staff of the BCLT were actively involved in all of these legislative efforts to expand funding for affordable housing, as well as several unsuccessful campaigns to enact ordinances to protect the rights of vulnerable renters, including an anti-speculation tax and just-cause eviction.

There continued to be considerable overlap among city government, the emerging Progressive Party created by activists who had helped to elect Bernie Sanders, and the BCLT. The BCLT's first executive director was Tim McKenzie, a neighborhood activist

> Conservationists and housing
> advocates united in their
> opposition to the threat of
> unfettered land speculation.

who had helped to mobilize voter support for Bernie's first successful campaigns for mayor. Gretchen Bailey, an Assistant City Attorney who had been one of Bernie's first hires, conducted much of the legal research that enabled the BCLT to craft a ground lease compatible with Vermont law. The first board president of the BCLT was Brenda Torpy, who served as the City's housing director until moving to a job at the Vermont Housing Finance Agency. Torpy was followed in the housing director's job by John Davis, the former employee from ICE who had assisted CEDO in establishing the BCLT. When Tim McKenzie stepped down as the BCLT's executive director in 1991, Torpy was hired as his successor, assuming leadership of the organization she had helped to establish seven years before.

Burlington was the fulcrum and the leader of the effort in Vermont to make permanent affordability the cornerstone of all housing policy. In the 1980s, when affordability restrictions began expiring on federally subsidized, privately owned rental housing that had been built twenty years earlier, Vermont was one of the states hit the hardest by the threatened loss of this affordable housing. At the same time, an overheated real estate market was causing a steep rise in the price of for-sale, owner-occupied housing throughout Vermont. These twin crises allowed advocates to bring the CLT model and other progressive housing solutions to the attention of the Vermont legislature. With the support of both the legislature and Governor Madeline Kunin, advocates were successful in incorporating a priority for permanent affordability into an increasing number of state laws and plans.

During this same period, Vermont began experiencing a wave of speculative development in the countryside that threatened its traditional agricultural landscape. Conservationists and housing advocates found themselves united in their opposition to the threat of unfettered land speculation, luxury development, and gentrification. An outcome of this convergence of interests and concerns was a powerful coalition of affordable housing providers, conservationists, and preservationists who convinced the state legislature and the Kunin Administration in 1987 to create and to fund the Vermont Housing and Conservation Board (VHCB).[4] This quasi-public entity was funded by a portion of Vermont's property-transfer tax, money that was then used by VHCB to preserve open space, working farms, historic landmarks, and affordable housing. The priority recipients of the grants disbursed by VHCB were a network of nonprofits doing land conservation or affordable housing that were obligated to steward these land-based resources permanently. Funding from VHCB helped to create and to sustain the operations and the projects of community land trusts in Burlington and throughout the state. Indeed, this new crop of CLTs became the principal means by which VHCB sought to accomplish its affordable housing mission.

The Burlington Community Land Trust was able to grow and to thrive in this favorable policy environment. With the government of its city and the government of its state both embracing the principle of permanent affordability — and both directing public capital toward projects and organizations that would make this principle a reality — the BCLT was able to turn a forward-thinking policy into the sticks and bricks of new housing.

BUILDING A DIVERSE PORTFOLIO OF PERMANENTLY AFFORDABLE HOUSING

The BCLT's original strategy was twofold: to expand homeownership by creating a resale-restricted, leased-land homeownership product/program that would be accepted by public funders, private lenders, and prospective homebuyers; and to improve the Old North End, a neighborhood with an aging housing stock that was in poor condition but losing its affordability because of the neighborhood's proximity to the downtown, the waterfront, and the University of Vermont.

On the homeownership side, the first challenge was to gain acceptance for the CLT model and, in particular, its separation of land and buildings. This dual-ownership model frightened lenders and daunted appraisers. There were few other CLTs to point to in the early 1980's. Thus there was no track record to reassure skeptical lenders and public leaders that, first, there would be a market for limited-equity homes on leased land, and second, that the benefits would outweigh the risks to either buyers or lenders. Even Bernie Sanders worried, at first, that this might be "second class homeownership for working people."

The BCLT also faced the wrath of private realtors and for-profit developers who objected strenuously to the removal of land and housing from the speculative market. A few years after the organization was established, some of them organized Homeowners Against the Land Trust (HALT) to oppose a proposed BCLT development in which single-family detached houses were to be built on donated land. They picketed City Hall, singing "Oh give me a home with land that I own," to the tune of *Home, Home on the Range.*

This was a stark reminder that what the BCLT was committed to doing was a scary departure from business as usual. Burlington's progressive government may have embraced permanent affordability as a necessary response to the inequities of a profit-oriented housing market and as a way to retain the value of the public investment in housing, but that didn't mean that the private sector — or the NIMBYs living near BCLT housing — were ready to do so.[5]

The BCLT appealed for help to the Vermont Housing Finance Agency (VHFA), a state agency that had been established to provide mortgages for first-time homebuyers. After much hemming and hawing, VHFA accepted the CLT model, but only half-way. VHFA's solution for persuading their participating banks to chance this new thing was to create a rider to the ground lease, which gave banks the option of taking the entire property (land and home) if the BCLT did not cure a mortgage default in a specified time. The BCLT's leadership was confident of prevailing and never letting a property go to foreclosure, so

> Local bankers became ardent supporters when they saw there were virtually no foreclosures.

they reluctantly agreed to this bargain, at least until the model was proven. Later, a more favorable arrangement was negotiated that protected BCLT's interest in the entire property. No longer was BCLT required to pledge its land as collateral when a homeowner obtained a mortgage through VHFA. Once VHFA was on board, the BCLT was able to engage with local bankers who eventually became ardent supporters — especially when they saw there were virtually no foreclosures among the low-income homeowners being served by the land trust.

The first home purchased by the BCLT was a vacant, single-family house. It had been spotted by a single mother, an assistant librarian named Kathy Neilson who happened to attend a public forum at the library introducing the BCLT. She wanted a decent, secure home in which to raise her two daughters, so Kathy volunteered to be the "guinea pig" for the new model of tenure that the land trust was trying to establish.

As the BCLT's founders continued to worry their way through all the policies and structures for the new CLT and continued to negotiate with VHFA to create a mortgage product for resale-restricted homes on leased land, Kathy and her daughters cleaned up the site of what she hoped would be her new home. By autumn, she told the new BCLT board: "I mowed the grass all summer, and I'm raking the leaves now, but I will *not* plow the snow unless I am living there." Goaded by this passionate, prospective homebuyer who was growing a bit impatient with how long it was taking to put a roof over her head, the BCLT's leaders speeded up their efforts. All the pieces were pulled together and BCLT had its first closing in 1985. Kathy Neilson got her home at last — before the winter.

Since then, over 234 single-family houses have been placed under the CLT's stewardship, along with 372 condominiums and 5 duplexes. All of these owner-occupied homes are encumbered with permanent contractual restrictions that ensure they will be resold in the future to income-eligible households for an affordable price. The BCLT's ongoing stewardship of this owner-occupied housing — a portfolio currently totaling over 600 homes — also prevents absentee ownership, deferred maintenance, and predatory lending, while allowing the CLT to intervene (if necessary) to prevent foreclosures.

From its earliest days, the BCLT strategically purchased small, multi-family rental properties containing two to six housing units in the Old North End to avert tenant displacement. The initial plan was to work with existing tenants to convert these properties into limited-equity cooperatives, but over time the BCLT came to realize that larger multi-unit buildings were more likely to succeed as cooperatives. *Converting* existing rental housing into a cooperative was much harder to do (and less likely to succeed) than *constructing* a new building and organizing a new group of residents to create a cooperative association from scratch. There are now six limited-equity and zero-equity housing cooperatives in the organization's portfolio, containing a total of 121 co-op apartments.

On the neighborhood development side of its mission, the BCLT quickly evolved beyond its initial anti-gentrification commitment to the Old North End. By the 1990s,

Fig. 2.3. Celebration of CHT's 500th owner-occupied home, 2011. Featured in photo: CHT executive director, Brenda Torpy (l), former Mayor, Bob Kiss (c), and Vermont Housing and Conservation Board executive director, Gus Seelig (r).

the BCLT possessed a growing portfolio of rental housing and had already started to build its internal capacity to be a good social landlord. At first, it managed a relatively small number of scattered-site, rehabilitated rental properties, primarily in the Old North End. Over time, it expanded its service area beyond the Old North End and also began developing affordable rental housing, making use of Low Income Housing Tax Credits, a new federal program that provided equity for the construction or rehabilitation of housing served tenant households below 60% of Area Median Income. By the end of 2019, the community land trust owned and managed 2,431 rental apartments.

A LARGER GEOGRAPHY AND A BROADER MISSION

The BCLT had been founded with a city-wide focus, confining its activities during its first years to housing development within Burlington's boundaries. The BCLT expanded its service area in 1987 to include all of Chittenden County. In 2001, it expanded even further to cover the three northwest counties of Vermont, bordering Lake Champlain on the west and Canada to the north. This three-county service area encompasses 1,506 square miles, with a total population of 217,042 people. At the request of town governments within that area, the BCLT began to construct new rental housing and to operate a regional housing rehabilitation loan program for low-income homeowners.

The BCLT's greatest change and biggest leap came in 2005, when the leaders of the Lake Champlain Housing Development Corporation (LCHDC) invited the staff and board of the BCLT to explore a formal alliance and, possibly, a merger. By that time, decades of HUD cutbacks and a draconian shredding of the social safety net by a succession of federal administrations were putting both nonprofits at risk. A Republican Governor in Montpelier posed a threat to housing development funds coming from the state as well.[6] It no longer seemed feasible for LCHDC and the BCLT to share a relatively small service area and to compete for a scarce supply of dollars, sites, and political support. LCHDC possessed about 1,200 rental apartments. The BCLT's holdings included about 700 homes, divided equally between homeownership and rentals. Neither portfolio was large enough to be truly sustainable.

After a year of conversation, negotiation, and planning, the two organizations decided to merge into one. The BCLT was chosen to be the surviving corporation due to its strong membership base, broad donor support, and the diversity of its programs and funding sources. The name chosen for the newly merged corporation was the Champlain Housing Trust (CHT).

The model of membership and governance of a "classic" CLT was embraced by both boards during the negotiations leading up to the merger. Champlain Housing Trust continued to be structured as a membership organization with a tri-partite board, although that structure was modified slightly to incorporate LCHDC's strong link to the municipal governments that had created LCHDC back in 1984. Five seats on the governing board were reserved for homeowners, renters, or co-op members living in one of the homes in CHT's portfolio. Five seats were reserved for representatives of CHT's general membership: people who live within CHT's service area and support CHT's mission, but who do not live in a CHT home. Five seats were reserved for officials from the public sector, drawn from various municipal governments and regional bodies within CHT's three-county service area.

In the financial crisis of 2008, Vermont did not experience a crash in real estate values, but the state was hit hard by the subsequent economic downturn, producing a startling, multi-year rise in homelessness. Shelters and homeless assistance programs sponsored by the state government were overwhelmed and sought CHT's assistance. This was not an entirely new activity for CHT, but the scope of its role grew substantially in response to this crisis. CHT's ability to rapidly finance and develop properties enabled CHT to promptly create a new homeless facility, a converted motel where individuals and families could be temporarily housed and have access to services provided on-site. The success of this project led to CHT's most recent contribution to the region's housing needs: a partnership with the University of Vermont Medical Center Hospital to house people who are chronically ill and homeless. The Hospital has contributed three million dollars in capital, along with operating subsidies for on-site health services at two housing sites, enabling CHT to work towards its goal of eliminating chronic homelessness.

Over the years, the land trust has gradually added a number of non-residential projects to its portfolio as well. Beginning in the 1990s, the BCLT assumed a broader community development role in the Old North End: redeveloping polluted sites and returning abandoned and blighted properties to community use. BCLT not only built housing. It also developed a pocket park, a food shelf, a multi-generational community center, and buildings for nonprofit offices delivering everything from affordable health care to legal services. A former bus barn was converted into commercial spaces for a neighborhood restaurant, a laundromat, a garage for repairing and recycling cars, and a shop for repairing and selling bicycles. Since the 2006 merger, CHT has developed downtown office spaces, including a multi-story, mixed-use building in which CHT is headquartered. At present, organization's real estate portfolio contains over 160,000 square feet of nonresidential space.

Fig. 2.4. Vermont Transit bus barn, rehabilitated and re-purposed for neighborhood retail.

CHT's most recent non-housing venture is the acquisition and rehabilitation of a former Catholic elementary school in the Old North End, which had been mostly vacant for many years. CHT converted the building into a thriving community center. An anchor tenant is the City's Parks and Recreation Department, which is making full use of the building's gym for year-around recreation and sports, and also hosting arts and cultural activities and a daily senior center. Sharing the building with Parks and Recreation are a family center, a cooperative child development center, an amateur theatre, and a non-profit organization providing refugees and New Americans with legal, health and social services, job training, youth services, translation, and English language classes. A large community room and a commercial kitchen accommodate neighborhood meetings and provide an affordable space for family gatherings like weddings and memorials, as well as for cultural celebrations and festivals.

CHT's ever-expanding array of projects and services requires a large staff. A hundred employees oversee a diverse real estate portfolio that, in addition to several nonresidential buildings, currently contains over 3000 homes. CHT's residential holdings include shelters for the homeless, community homes with built-in services, rental apartments, limited-equity cooperatives, limited-equity condominiums, co-housing, and resale-restricted houses on leased land, providing a continuum of housing options for low-income and moderate-income households. CHT's staff provides a rich mix of services

Fig. 2.5. Participants in the international study visit sponsored by World Habitat, 2009.

A hundred employees oversee a diverse real estate portfolio of over 3000 homes.

for homeowners and renters alike, helping them to succeed in the housing that is theirs and enabling them to move along this continuum to achieve the type and tenure of housing that is best for them. These services include financial education and counselling for applicants seeking to rent, purchase, or retain housing, as well as case management for those with special needs. Staff support is also provided for community-building activities like gardens and youth programs.

In 2008, CHT received the United Nations World Habitat Award for the Global North, recognizing the fiscal, environmental, and social sustainability of the community land trust model. This brought international attention and acclaim for CHT's distinctive approach to the decommodification of housing. As a component of that award, CHT hosted an "international study visit" in June 2009 with participants from thirteen countries. The peer-to-peer relationships formed during this visit helped to hasten the spread of the CLT model to other countries, including Australia, Belgium, and the United Kingdom. More recently CHT has established connections with fledgling CLTs in Canada and France.

Meanwhile, back in the USA, the Champlain Housing Trust has continued to be a leader in state-wide housing coalitions in Vermont and is also heavily invested at the national level in supporting the Grounded Solutions Network. GSN provides training, technical assistance, and advocacy for CLTs and other organizations that are dedicated to creating housing with affordability that lasts. This is precisely the principle that CHT has championed for over thirty-five years, believing that the best things in life truly *are* perpetually affordable.

Notes

1. At one point, CHT's board president was a registered Republican who was proud to advocate for CHT's model because of its adherence to the "republican" virtue of thrifty public spending.

2. The BCLT— and, later, CHT— was the first community land trust in the USA to conduct longitudinal studies evaluating the model's performance, providing quantitative evidence that stewardship works. See: Davis and Demetrowitz, 2003; Davis and Stokes, 2008.

3. Burlington's inclusionary zoning (IZ) ordinance, enacted in 1990, requires developers to earmark a specified percentage of the units in a newly constructed or substantially rehabilitated housing project, units that must be offered for rent or sale at a below-market price. This percentage ranges from 15% to 25%, depending on the zoning district in which the project is located. The City has the first option to purchase all IZ units, an option that is often assigned to BCLT/CHT, bringing new units into the land trust's portfolio of permanently affordable housing.

4. More about VHCB — and its legislatively mandated commitment to permanent afford-ability — can be found in an essay by Jim Libby (2010).

5. Opposition from homeowners who live near a proposed housing project is a common occurrence in cities and suburbs in the United States, especially when a project is slated to be occupied by persons whose income is lower or whose skin is darker than most of the neighborhood's current residents. Among city planners and affordable housing advo-cates, these opponents are often characterized as "NIMBYs," an acronym for "Not in My Back Yard."

6. Vermont elected a Republican Governor in 2002, Jim Douglas, who served until 2010. During this period, funding for VHCB continued, but advocates for affordable housing and land conservation were called upon again and again to defend VHCB in the legis-lature against proposals from the Governor to reduce VHCB funds or to redirect funds toward for-profit developers. BCLT played a key role in these legislative fights, stepping forward as one of VHCB's most vocal and persuasive defenders. The success of BCLT's projects, programs, and published evaluations helped to demonstrate the effectiveness of VHCB's priority for investing in projects with permanent affordability.

References

Champlain Housing Trust website: *http://www.getahome.org/*

John Emmeus Davis, "Building the Progressive City." Pp. 165–200 in J.E. Davis (ed.), *The Affordable City* (Philadelphia PA: Temple University Press, 1994). Available at: *https://ecommons.cornell.edu/handle/1813/40513*

John Emmeus Davis and Amy Demetrowitz, *Permanently Affordable Homeownership: Does the Community Land Trust Deliver on Its Promises?* (Burlington VT: Burlington Community Land Trust, 2003).

John Emmeus Davis and Alice Stokes, *Lands in Trust, Homes That Last.* (Burlington VT: Champlain Housing Trust, 2008). Available at: *http:/www.burlingtonassociates.com/#!/resources*

Jim Libby, "The Challenge of Perpetuity." Pp. 552–561 in J.E. Davis (ed.), *The Community Land Trust Reader* (Cambridge MA: The Lincoln Institute of Land Policy, 2010).

Kenneth Tempkin, Brett Theodos, and David Price. *Shared Equity Homeownership Evaluation: Case Study of Champlain Housing Trust.* (Washington, DC: The Urban Institute, 2010). Available at: *http://www.urban.org/uploadedpdf/412243-CHT.pdf*

Brenda Torpy, "The Community Land Trust Solution: The Case of the Champlain Housing Trust." Pp. 64–66 in Christopher Niedt and Mark Silver (eds.), *Forging a New Housing Policy: Opportunity in the Wake of Crisis* (National Center for Suburban Studies, Hofstra University, 2010).

3.

Stewardship of Urban Real Estate for Long-Term Community Benefit
Profile of the Urban Land Conservancy in Denver, Colorado

Alan Gottlieb and Aaron Miripol

The Urban Land Conservancy (ULC) was established in 2003 as a nonprofit corporation with a service area encompassing the Denver metropolitan area. Since then, ULC has grown and evolved to the point that it is now a major player in Denver's real estate scene. Its influence extends beyond the number of acres it owns and the number of developments it has sponsored. An integral part of both its internal success and its wider influence also comes from the organization's early adoption of key features of the community land trust (CLT).

ULC is not a traditional CLT. It actively involves community residents in planning its developments, but ULC does not have a community-based membership that elects a majority of its governing board. Unlike most CLTs in the United States, moreover, ULC's development of affordable housing has not included homeownership. Nevertheless, by any other measure, ULC has exemplified and championed the CLT model to a degree that few organizations have matched. ULC owns land in perpetuity. It strategically uses 99-year ground leases to preserve prime pieces of land in multiple neighborhoods facing the pressures of gentrification, ensuring the availability of those lands for the lasting benefit of low-income people in a booming real estate market. Its ground leases provide ULC with a legal mechanism for ensuring the permanent affordability of its place-based investments in multi-family rental housing and nonprofit facilities.

ULC is a unique organization with a singular history. We will review the organization's origins and describe the major projects that ULC has developed using the CLT model. We will also examine how ULC emphasizes and involves community, even though ULC's organizational structure differs significantly from that of a traditional CLT. Finally, we will consider what the future holds for CLT development in Metro Denver, as ULC incubates the Elevation CLT, a new organization that will be structured and operated along lines of the "classic" community land trust.

FROM IDEA TO EXECUTION

It was 2003 when the pieces of a puzzle snapped into place for Denver oilman Sam Gary. A philanthropist who had founded the Piton Foundation as well the Gary-Williams Energy Corporation, Gary had long admired how nonprofits like the Trust for Public Land and Colorado Open Lands acquired land in beautiful places to ensure the parcels would always provide a public benefit.

Why, he wondered, couldn't something similar be done with land in cities where real estate costs are rapidly escalating? Shouldn't there be a way to acquire urban land to ensure that any investment in the preservation of existing buildings or the development of new buildings would accrue as a lasting benefit to the public? In Gary's words:

> I developed my understanding of the value of land conservation early on, in the open lands conservation movement. I broadened my focus from open lands to urban lands. That sensibility converged with my desire to strengthen our urban communities where our most underserved children and families live.

As the funder of a philanthropic foundation, Gary had also grown frustrated with the struggles of nonprofits to buy buildings for the purpose of housing their own operations, only to see those properties occasionally lost to bank foreclosure when a nonprofit organization hit financial difficulties down the road.

After Sam Gary's epiphany, the leadership of his charitable foundation and his energy company began working together to flesh out his idea of creating a structure for acquiring and holding urban land for public benefit. Initially, Gary favored creating a land bank inside the Piton Foundation. But over time, he was persuaded that something more robust was needed. He realized, according to his nephew, Tim Howard, that "starting an organization that had a good mission and a sustainable operating model was a better way to go than creating a new program area within a small private foundation."

Tim Howard, despite his employment on the oil exploration side of the Gary-Williams Energy Corporation, had an abiding interest in helping Gary to create a land bank inside the Piton Foundation. He was given the assignment of putting together a plan for the nascent ULC and running the organization while a board was being put together and as ULC was getting off the ground.

"You can imagine a line of army recruits standing there," wryly commented Howard years later. "The drill sergeant says, 'all volunteers take one step forward,' and everyone takes one steps back except one guy who didn't quite hear the instructions. I was that guy."

Howard was a quick study, but he had no background in community development. Thanks to the deep connections within Denver's real estate community that Gary and his staff had formed over decades of philanthropic endeavors, however, ULC was able to assemble a powerhouse board of real estate developers, finance experts, and local philanthropists to oversee its operations, even before the organization officially existed.

The board's first chair was Tom Gougeon, who in the 1980s had served as a senior aide to Denver Mayor Federico Peña. He went on to head the Stapleton Redevelopment Foundation, leading the planning for what would be built on the massive site of Denver's old airport. He later became a private real estate developer, which was his role when he took the helm of the ULC board. He currently serves as president of the Gates Family Foundation in Denver. He recalls:

> We starting thinking about whether there was room for a land trust equivalent focused on the urban marketplace. It was a broader and different idea than the CLT model. It was more than housing. It was really this all-purpose real estate agent that could go out and intervene in the marketplace on behalf of the community. We were interested in schools and nonprofit space, health, and parks.

Conversations ensued with the Denver Foundation, a local community foundation, which adopted ULC as a "supporting organization" and provided ULC with administrative and accounting services during its first decade, while managing ULC's cash as a donor-advised fund. The Foundation also appointed half the members of ULC's board, a practice that has continued to the present. Otherwise the Foundation does not intervene in ULC's development decisions or in its day-to-day operations.

ULC GROWS UP

In its early years, with no staff, ULC operated in an opportunistic fashion, pursuing attractive real estate deals as they became available. Susan Powers, a Denver-based developer and former head of the Denver Urban Renewal Authority who served on the inaugural ULC board, recalled developing with Tom Gougeon and with other members of the board a list of projects they'd like to pursue.

The new organization got a major boost in 2007, when the Gary-Williams Energy Corporation donated three properties to ULC, together valued at more than $7 million. This included the Tramway Building, occupying a square block in the low-income Cole neighborhood, and a former Budget Motel in northeast Denver, leased to the Colorado Coalition for the Homeless serving families coming out of homelessness. The Corporation also endowed ULC with a donation of cash to leverage other real estate purchases. There were no written restrictions placed on how the money could be used. Susan Powers later recalled the feeling of amazement that came over them in that moment:

> Then one day Sam Gary said he wanted to have a phone call with me and Tom, and on that call he told us he wanted to give us $10 million. Obviously, it was extremely generous, and it meant that we weren't going to be a land conservancy starting from scratch. But it did make us wonder how we were going to do this as a group of volunteers.

Gary's largess prompted ULC's board to decide that the time had come to hire a full-time president & chief executive officer. The board launched a national search. Several board members were already familiar with Aaron Miripol or knew him by reputation. Miripol had been running Thistle Community Housing in Boulder County since 1998. Thistle was a community development corporation that had established, developed, and administered a successful CLT as an internal program, one of only two CLTs in Colorado at the time.

Miripol, a CLT expert and an evangelist for the model, had impressed Sam Gary, Tim Howard and others from Gary-Williams and the Piton Foundation during an earlier trip they had taken to Boulder to learn about Thistle's CLT. "Aaron gets a lot of credit for really pushing forward the CLT concept. So when it came time to hire a leader for ULC, he was the first person I thought of," Howard said.

The rest of the board agreed. Miripol took the helm of the ULC in mid-2007. In Howard's estimation, time has proven the wisdom of the board's choice:

> ULC would be another one of those nonprofits that the foundation community tried to start and get off the ground but somehow wasn't sustainable if Aaron hadn't taken that job. The key is the overlap between his belief in and understanding of permanent stewardship through the CLT and all the different manifestations it has to take to adapt to different community needs. That and the fact that he is like an energizer bunny. His go-go ability to get stuff done and motivate people, whether partners or his staff, is a unique thing that has allowed ULC to succeed.

COMMUNITY LAND TRUST PROJECTS, 2007–2019

After being hired by ULC, Miripol's first task was to build the organization's internal capacity to manage the properties donated by Sam Gary and to begin planning and developing large-scale projects. In the ensuing years, ULC has gone from a staff of one to a staff of 17 full-time employees.

One of Miripol's enduring contributions to ULC has been his ability to attract and hire high-quality staff, with both knowledge of the development field and passion for the work. It's the strength of the staff from top to bottom that provides ULC with sufficient capacity to do such a high volume of excellent work. The extraordinarily strong, committed staff makes ULC a true, mission-driven organization.

By 2019, the organization had overseen the development of eight major projects using the CLT model, representing a total investment of $37 million in equity. Five of these CLT projects are described below. They provide insight into the diversity of ULC's activities and the versatility of doing equitable and sustainable development on community-owned land.

Jody Apartments, Housing Preservation Near Public Transit

ULC's first CLT investment was the $725,000 purchase in 2007 of two acres of land under Jody Apartments, an existing 62-unit rental housing complex serving lower-income households located on Denver's western border. These apartments are next to a stop on the light rail line of the Regional Transportation District (RTD), connecting downtown Denver to the western suburb of Golden.

NEWSED, a community development corporation that has operated in Denver since 1973, had wanted to buy the property with the intention of rehabilitating the four buildings and preserving them as affordable housing. NEWSED initially approached ULC to ask about receiving a construction loan. ULC declined. Instead, hewing to its mission, ULC used its investment to buy the land underneath Jody Apartments, while NEWSED continued to own and to manage these buildings as rental housing.

NEWSED leases the land from ULC through a 99-year ground lease. Under the terms of the ground lease, 52 of the 62 apartments must remain permanently affordable. Twelve of the 52 are reserved for extremely low-income households (families earning $20,000 or less per year).

More recently, ULC acquired four additional acres adjacent to both Jody Apartments and the light rail station, thereby maximizing the opportunity to provide permanently affordable housing and nonprofit facilities at the site. Development is underway on the first phase. ULC is partnering with two for-profit affordable housing developers, Brinshore Development and Mile High, in building Sheridan Station Residences, 133 permanently affordable apartments atop a 99-year ground lease with ULC. Ultimately, the balance of the four-acre site will provide 250 additional affordable homes, along with up to 50,000 feet of commercial space.

Holly Square Shopping Center

ULC's highest-profile and most impactful CLT investment to date has been the redevelopment of the Holly Square shopping center in the historically African-American neighborhood of Northeast Park Hill.[1] The Holly, as it is widely known, was formerly a center of Denver's African-American community, and a source of pride for many. In its heyday, from the mid-1950s to mid-1970s, the shopping center was anchored by a Safeway supermarket, and also featured a barber shop, a hardware store, a dentistry office, a general apparel store, a dry cleaner, a variety store and a candy store, among other small businesses. Many of these enterprises were owned by African-Americans.

When the supermarket closed in the mid 1970s, The Holly began to deteriorate. Its anchor space remained vacant for several years until the Hope Center, a local nonprofit, purchased the supermarket for its home in 1979. Then, in the late 1980s, on the heels of the crack cocaine epidemic that swept the nation, local affiliates of Los Angeles street gangs arrived on the scene. A newspaper article described The Holly of the late 1980s as "home base for the Park Hill Bloods."

The center hit its nadir in May 2008, when a rival gang firebombed The Holly in retaliation for the fatal shooting of one of its leaders. The burned-out center could have become a blighted eyesore, casting a pall over the surrounding area. Instead, community leaders vowed to replace it with something better.

After city officials initiated conversations about The Holly's future with Aaron Miripol, ULC bought the 2.6-acre property for $625,000, part of which was covered by a $200,000 forgivable loan from the City of Denver. Working together, community residents, city officials, the Denver Foundation, and ULC created a participatory community-planning process known as the Holly Area Redevelopment Project (HARP).

Members of the HARP steering committee gathered input from neighborhood residents about the kinds of services, programs, and businesses that should occupy the space.[2] What ultimately resulted was a plan for the complete transformation of Holly Square, anchored by a new Boys & Girls Club and a public elementary school, housed within new buildings that sit atop land that is owned by ULC.

The Boys & Girls Club has a 99-year land lease with ULC, which will automatically renew for another 99 years. The Boys & Girls Club paid ULC for development rights that were 75 percent below market-rate with annual land-lease payments to ULC of less than $5,000 per year. The development fee paid off ULC's debt on the land and a portion of its holding costs.

Fig. 3.1. The new Boys & Girls Club at Holly Square.

Unfortunately, the Roots Elementary School closed in 2019 due to low enrollment, caused in part by poor educational performance. However, because ULC still owns the land under the Roots building, ULC is leading the negotiations with interested nonprofits who want to call the Holly their home.

The shopping center also has an adjacent public library and city recreation center, making it a true hub of the community. The former head of Roots Elementary called The Holly a "mini Harlem Children's Zone." Thanks to the land leases, both the Boys & Girls

Club and the former school facilities will remain community assets far into the future. This is a lasting community benefit, described by Miripol as follows:

> We want to be good stewards of the Holly property, and one way of doing that is protecting the future use through our CLT 99-year ground leases. When you combine what HARP has done with all of the positive changes taking place at Dahlia (another recently redeveloped shopping center in the neighborhood), you have a number of impactful assets, all of them important pieces of a vibrant community.

Curtis Park Community Center

ULC purchased the vacant Curtis Park Community Center in 2012 for $600,000 from the American Baptist Church of the Rocky Mountain Region. The purchase price was partially offset by a $350,000 forgivable loan from the City of Denver. The center is located in the heart of the Curtis Park neighborhood, a rapidly gentrifying area filled with stately Victorian homes.

Fig. 3.2. Playground, Family Star Montessori.

ULC entered into an agreement to revitalize the site with a venerable early childhood program, Family Star Montessori, which serves children from low-income families. ULC partnered with Family Star in completing $1.2 million in renovations that were needed to open the school. In 2017, Family Star bought the renovated building from ULC for $885,000, with a 99-year ground lease for the underlying land. Family Star makes annual lease payments of $7,000 to help compensate ULC for the roughly $750,000 that ULC "left in the land." These lease payments provide ULC with a one percent return on its investment in the land. ULC plays a unique role in not only ensuring the nonprofit's beneficial use of the property, but also providing opportunities for mission-driven organizations to become anchors in their communities.

New Legacy Charter School

The New Legacy Charter School Project provides another example of how land ownership has allowed ULC to preserve and, in this case, to create important community assets. New Legacy is a small charter high school designed to serve teen parents and their children. The school is home to a fully licensed infant-through-early-childhood center, so that teen parents can attend classes knowing their children are close at hand and safe in an enriching environment.

Before the school existed, its founder approached ULC for help in finding a facility in NW Aurora, a low-income section of Denver's largest inner-ring suburb. After a few failed attempts to secure a facility, ULC purchased a vacant bowling alley in 2014 for $675,000 with plans to convert it to a school. Ultimately, ULC and New Legacy decided that a better solution would be to demolish the building and to start fresh. The result was a new, gleaming 23,000 square-foot school building that opened in the fall of 2015. It was made possible by the creative financing assembled by ULC.

After protracted negotiations, the school and ULC agreed on a formula for determining rent payments for the building. Under the terms of the lease, New Legacy has an option to purchase the building from ULC upon expiration of the original five-year agreement (in 2020). Should the school eventually buy the building, ULC will retain ownership of the land, conveying the site to the school through a renewable 99-year ground lease.

The Site at 38th and Blake Streets

In 2011, ULC purchased two abandoned buildings out of foreclosure at 38th Street and Blake Street for $1.7 million ($26/square foot), just ahead of a real estate boom in the Cole neighborhood that has seen the land's value appreciate by 500 percent. This 1.5-acre site, adjacent to the Blake Street Station on RTD's light rail line, was purchased using Denver's Transit Oriented Development (TOD) Fund. The site is located on the edge of Cole, a working-class community caught in a vise between the booming, gentrified River North neighborhood and a massive reconstruction of Interstate 70 running through central Denver.

ULC had originally envisioned developing a five-story residential building on the site, providing 114 income-restricted units. However, ULC's partner, Medici Consulting Group (MCG), was denied twice by the Colorado Housing and Finance Authority (CHFA) when it applied for tax credits for the project, due to fierce statewide competition for the credits. Following the second rejection, ULC opted to split its holdings into two parcels: 3789 Walnut Street and 3750 Blake Street. MCG then applied successfully for tax credits for the Walnut Street Lofts and ULC began working to sell the Blake Street site to another developer.

In March 2019, MCG broke ground on 66 units of permanently affordable housing at the corner of 38th and Walnut on the southeast side of the property, providing one-, two- and three-bedroom units for households earning 30%-60% of the Area Median Income. In addition, the property will join ULC's growing community land trust through the implementation of a 99-year renewable ground lease agreement to ensure the property remains affordable in perpetuity.

In selling the other parcel, ULC negotiated with a developer to include at least 30 income-restricted units, 11 more than was required by the City's zoning overlay. In addition, ULC negotiated a First Right of Refusal (at a below-market price) to purchase the

Fig. 3.3. Before and after: the site at 38th and Blake Streets when first acquired by ULC in 2011 (top); a rendering of the rental housing built on the site (bottom).

30 units if the owner were to decide in the future to convert the rental building into for-sale condos.

Together, the 3789 Walnut Street and 3750 Blake Street parcels will provide 96 permanently affordable, income-restricted apartments. The proceeds from the sale of the Blake Street lot to the developer also allowed ULC to plan for additional affordable housing four blocks away at Cole Train, next to the Tramway Nonprofit Center.

The Site at 48th Avenue and Race Street

ULC purchased a six-acre site at East 48th Avenue and Race Street in April 2015 for $5.5 million with loans from the City of Denver and the Calvert Impact Fund. The Colorado Health Foundation provided additional funding to support healthy design and development. The site is located near a new, soon-to-be-opened commuter rail station in Elyria-Swansea, a neighborhood that was cut in two in the early 1960s by the construction of Interstate 70. The area is home to a number of industrial sites and adjacent to the National Western Stock Show. The latter is being redeveloped into a year-round tourist destination. It will also provide new and improved multi-modal pathways to reconnect Elyria and Swansea, bringing life back into these communities.

In 2018, after conducting a year-long community engagement process to create designs for future development, ULC announced that Columbia Ventures LLC would be its development partner for the $150 million project on ULC's six-acre site. Plans include both permanently affordable housing and market-rate housing, as well as the construction of 50,000 square feet of community commercial space.

This development project will also provide a new home for Clinica Tepayac, a 25-year-old nonprofit health clinic providing culturally competent health services for the medically underserved. Clinica Tepayac's 25,000 square-foot facility will become part of ULC's community land trust to ensure long-term community benefit. With the recent award of federal and state tax credits,[3] 150 permanently affordable apartments will be built above Clinica's new health clinic. The eventual completion of all parts of this transit-oriented development at 48th and Race will more than quadruple the supply of permanently affordable housing in the neighborhood.

HOW ULC PUTS THE "C" IN CLT

The Urban Land Conservancy is not a typical community land trust. Many CLTs across the country are formed to work in a single neighborhood, with a sole focus on homeownership. That is not the case with the ULC, which has acquired and developed multiple properties across the Denver metropolitan area and does no homeownership. All of the housing on its lands are multi-unit rentals. As Tom Gougeon has noted:

> ULC never was going to be built on the classic homeownership land trust model: community grass-rootsy, advocacy-based organizations. This is partly because of the small geography of those organizations, compared to the ULC's geographical scope.

It is also the case that most CLTs across the country are overseen by a board with significant representation from the people who live in the CLT's properties. Because ULC has not done homeownership, it does not have the same representation. Instead, board members are chosen from the community for their expertise in development, law, finance and/or government. The complexity of the organization and the variety of its projects makes an expertise-based board a necessity. Again, according to Tom Gougeon:

> If you think about what ULC has been doing, it is a much more sophisticated operation with a broader set of skills required than even a good-sized CLT. ULC projects include housing, yes, but also office buildings and retail space and schools. They all have different financing structures and regulatory structures, and are spread across many municipalities. That is why you need a board with the attributes of ULC's board. You may not

need all of that in a traditional CLT, which leaves more room for resident representation. ULC is a kindred enterprise to a CLT, but an outlier because of those factors.

Still, ULC puts significant effort into community involvement. The clearest example is the Holly Square redevelopment, where the Holly Area Redevelopment Project committee included significant community representation. HARP members chose the partners that ultimately occupied the property.

In the summer of 2018, ULC hired two "managers of neighborhood partnerships" to oversee the organization's work in communities where it owns properties. Both individuals have deep roots in Metro Denver neighborhoods, and extensive experience in community organizing.

"Hiring them was critical to building stronger relationships with community stakeholders," Miripol said. "That was an area where we hadn't had the capacity we needed." In 2018, ULC added a CLT committee to its organization. The committee consists of representatives from organizations that "own the improvements" on lands owned by ULC.

Why has it taken so long for ULC to create a CLT committee? According to Miripol, it takes a certain economy of scale to form such a committee. ULC currently has five CLT entities, with a sixth and seventh coming in the next year. In previous years, it wouldn't have made sense to form a CLT committee because there would have been few members, representing a small number of properties. But recent and upcoming growth in ULC's CLT properties made this the right time to put together a committee.

SUCCESSES AND CHALLENGES IN THE CLT REALM

From Aaron Miripol's perspective, ULC's most notable successes in the CLT realm have come when partners have understood the value to both parties of community-owned land and long-term ground leases. Conversely, the biggest challenges have arisen when there was a lack of understanding of the model used by ULC to preserve affordability and to protect community assets.

The Holly Shopping Center redevelopment is the jewel in ULC's community land trust crown. "It's a quintessential use of the CLT because stakeholders have confidence that the land will never go to market, regardless of what happens to the programs currently operating there," Miripol said. Indeed, the site will remain a hub of the community for 198 years, thanks to automatically renewing 99-year ground leases on the land under the Boys & Girls Club and the former Roots Elementary School.

In a similar vein, the Curtis Park Community Center purchase ensures long-term community benefit for a property in the heart of a neighborhood undergoing an inexorable transformation caused by gentrification. And the Jody Apartments will remain affordable in perpetuity, thanks to a long-term ground lease.

In all three cases, initial reluctance on the part of ULC's partners about entering into a ground lease rather than buying the land was overcome by the cost savings realized by not having to purchase the land.

Conversely, ULC's most challenging projects have been those where long-term ground leasing would have made sense but the projects' partners couldn't be persuaded that this approach would serve them better than owning the land. As Miripol explains:

> Even with our successes, there continues to be a lack of commitment to the use of CLTs. We have folks that struggle with the idea of ULC owning the land, as if it limits their ability to get full market rate in the future. Owning the land is a value we bring by taking the up-front risk of purchasing a property. We don't want to ever sell the land because we believe that regardless of whether you're the greatest nonprofit or for-profit developer, we don't know what a neighborhood is going to look like 20–30 years from now and what its changing needs will be.

Another challenge to expanding ULC's portfolio of community-owned land is Denver's real estate boom. Land is overpriced at the moment, making it difficult to do any kind of real estate deal, be it a CLT or something more traditional.

But it is at precisely such moments that an organization like ULC becomes so vital to maintaining the essential fabric of the community. According to Susan Powers, a private developer who served on ULC's board for a decade, "Timing is everything. ULC has to be the organization that looks well into the future and finds ways to keep projects alive when no one else can."

WHAT THE FUTURE HOLDS FOR ULC
AND CLT DEVELOPMENT IN COLORADO

The Urban Land Conservancy currently owns several parcels of land where it plans to employ CLT ground leases in future developments. One is the site of a former Thriftway supermarket in a low-income neighborhood in southwest Denver that is beginning to experience gentrification. ULC bought the property in 2014, demolished the building, and contracted with a local community organizing group to solicit deep community involvement in determining how the site should be redeveloped.

In 2016, following an intensive community engagement process, ULC completed construction of an interim pocket park and futsal court on the property. Long-term plans for the site are to do beneficial development that addresses the needs of the community. Through a future community engagement process, ULC will create a catalytic neighborhood asset for Westwood residents. One thing is certain: Whatever permanent facilities are built on the site will sit on land that ULC continues to own.

In the summer of 2018, ULC received its largest donation to date with the former Excelsior Youth Campus in Aurora, a 31-acre site that includes seventeen buildings. Now called Oxford Vista, the campus is headquarters for the Southwest Division of Americorps' National Community Conservation Corps. Another nonprofit, Family Tree, is leasing four buildings on the site to provide housing, early childhood education, and other services for families coming out of homelessness. ULC's long-term expectation is that the entire campus will be in a community land trust

Finally, ULC has played a leading role in starting the Elevation Community Land Trust (ECLT). In this case, ULC is developing an organization, rather than developing or redeveloping a parcel of land. Elevation CLT is a regional CLT that focuses on affordable homeownership. It is being incubated by ULC until the program can be spun off to become its own independent, tax-exempt, not-for-profit corporation.

"Elevation will provide all of the stewardship components related to homeownership like homebuyer counseling, which are services ULC doesn't provide," said Dave Younggren, President and CEO of Gary Community Investments and the Piton Foundation, the successor organization to Gary-Williams Energy Corporation.

Rather than being concentrated in a single neighborhood — or in a single city — Elevation CLT will use a scattered-site approach and have the flexibility to go to scale in any community at risk of gentrification and displacement. Its service area will eventually

Fig. 3.4. Aerial view of the 31-acre Oxford Vista site in Aurora, Colorado.

> Elevation CLT will have the flexibility to go to scale in any community at risk of gentrification and displacement.

expand beyond Denver Metro to support CLT homeownership across Colorado. To further support low-income families in the communities it serves, the Elevation CLT aims to align itself with comprehensive supportive services programs that provide residents with increased access to health care and healthy food, early childhood education, workforce training and placement, and wealth-building opportunities.

Elevation is being launched with a $24 million investment from a consortium of local philanthropic foundations, led by Gary Community Investments. Sam Gary's original vision for land ownership has now come full circle. It has ended up right back where it started — preserving urban land for community benefit.

Since its founding in 2003, ULC has made 37 real estate investments totaling over $120 million. Through its developments, ULC has leveraged an additional $700 million for the development of affordable housing (over 1,000 homes) and nonprofit facilities (700,000 square feet). Its projects have created more than 2,000 jobs. Its impact on the Denver metro area is undeniable. As Dave Younggren has observed:

> The community land trust as implemented by ULC has worked extremely well. The organization has done a remarkable job working in our community and is widely viewed as a real community resource and asset.

Controlling the land means controlling the impact and affordability of real estate, not only in the immediate future, but for multiple generations. It is important to think about how urban real estate fits into the fabric of community. ULC has proven how a CLT can ensure a positive impact in perpetuity.

Notes

1. A full history of the project can be found here: *https://www.urbanlandc.org/wp-content/uploads/2018/06/Holly-Final-reduced.pdf*

2. Staff from the Denver Foundation's Strengthening Neighborhoods initiative did much of the legwork of recruiting members for the HARP steering committee and ensuring that it represented the community's varied voices and interests.

3. Much of the equity raised by ULC for the recent development of three multi-family CLT projects — Sheridan Station, Walnut Lofts, and 48th & Race — has come from the Low Income Housing Tax Credit (LIHTC) program. This program was created in 1986 under Section 42 of the IRS Tax Code. It is currently the largest source of federal funding for the production of affordable rental housing. More than 900 units of housing have been built on ULC's sites using this program, roughly 80% of ULC's total affordable housing production.

4.

Origins and Evolution of Urban Community Land Trusts in Canada

Susannah Bunce and Joshua Barndt

The development of community land trusts in Canada offers an interesting study of the often individualized and ad hoc processes involved in CLT creation. While certainly not as numerous as CLTs in the USA and England, CLTs in Canada have burgeoned over the past several decades. They have been on the forefront of addressing affordable housing shortages and offered new ways to consider community land stewardship in Canada. The earliest CLTs were primarily located in Canadian cities, established as independent land trust initiatives through cooperative housing organizations, and as responses to affordable housing challenges in cities such as Montreal, Toronto, Winnipeg, and Vancouver. More recently, there has been an increasingly robust and more formalized network of CLTs emerging across Canada in response to on-going affordable housing shortages, gentrification processes, and a renewed interest in community-led practices that extend beyond affordable housing provision. Our chapter explores the historical appearance of CLTs in Canadian cities and why they continue to be an important community-led, non-governmental organizational model in a nation where government has traditionally played the leading role in the provision of affordable housing and social services.

Despite Canada's social democratic roots, different levels of government have been actively dismantling social programs over the last several decades, including a withdrawal from the funding and delivery of social housing programs starting in the early 1990s (Hulchanski 2001, 2007; Leone and Carole, 2010; Moore and Skaburskis, 2004; Wolfe, 1998).[1] Increasing governmental reliance on the private, for-profit sector for the delivery of housing and fiscal cutbacks to social services have had a detrimental impact on both housing affordability and the presence of social and community-based programs.[2]

Community-led CLT organizations have emerged within the context of these broader political-economic transformations in Canada, which have shaped the organizational structure, community actions, and programming of CLTs over time.

We identify two "generations" of community land trust organizations in Canada — the first being a small group of CLTs, arising in the 1980s to around 2012, that were largely focused on the acquisition of land for affordable housing provision. These CLT organizations, inspired by the CLT model in the United States, differed from land trust organizing in Canada that had traditionally focused on the conservation of wilderness and agricultural areas. The emergence of this new form of land trust in Canadian cities occurred within the context of a lack of public policy and legislative support for the creation of CLTs. As a result, they were primarily formed by cooperative housing federations, non-profit developers, and activist groups, often in partnership with specific governmental affordable housing programs.

A "second generation" of CLTs has emerged since 2012, both as a response to increasing gentrification pressures in urban areas and as a result of renewed interest in affordable housing development. New CLTs have emerged in cities such as Toronto and Vancouver,

> Canadian CLT development has been eclectic, sometimes incorporating features of the American model and sometimes not.

for example, cities that have experienced a steady rise in single-family homeownership and property speculation over the past decade, along with quickly rising housing prices and increased constraints on already tight affordable rental housing markets (Gee, 2017; King, 2016; McClearn, 2017). These second-generation CLTs have forged connections with existing and new CLT organizations across Canada and have interacted with an emergent international CLT movement. Locally, the activism of these CLT organizations has often extended beyond the land trust model itself, responding to broader urban issues such as the impact of rapid gentrification and displacement, decreases in affordable housing supply, advocacy for urban food security, and solidarity with racialized and culturally diverse communities, including building allyship with Indigenous peoples. These second-generation CLT organizations are distinguished by new approaches to the development and provision of communal and shared equity housing, by varied forms of neighbourhood and city-wide activism, and by a community land trust network being built across Canada.

Our chapter traces the evolution of Canadian CLTs and underlines the importance of their self-identification as CLTs in structuring their own organizations and operations. More often than not, Canadian CLT organizations view themselves as being a community land trust regardless of whether they exhibit all the characteristics of the traditional or "classic" CLT, as that model has been defined and implemented in the United States. The American "classic" model was premised on: a two-party ownership structure, whereby the CLT acts as the owner and long-term lessor for multiple parcels of land underneath buildings that are separately owned by individuals, cooperatives, or other nonprofit or for-profit entities; an organizational structure with a tripartite board and a place-based membership that emphasizes the participation of CLT residents, local community members, and members of the public; and an operational commitment to the permanent affordability of any housing located on the CLT's land, along with other stewardship duties designed to protect the condition of the structures and the security of tenure for the occupants (Davis, 2007; 2010). By comparison, Canadian CLT development has been more ad hoc and eclectic, sometimes incorporating these "classic" features and sometimes not, depending on their individual contexts and familiarity with the American CLT model. As such, Canadian CLTs have forged "home-grown" CLT characteristics that are primarily constituted by the very localized circumstances of their formation.

We trace the evolution of CLT development in Canada in a chronological way, through a narrative of the organizational objectives and projects of first- and second-generation CLTs. The CLTs that are discussed are organizations with which we are familiar, as CLT researchers and practitioners, and which offer certain insights into the origins and evolution of CLTs in the Canadian context. We conclude by suggesting that a steady increase in the presence of CLTs in Canada has necessitated the creation of formalized networks of knowledge transfer and information sharing in order to build solidarity and connections among CLT organizations and communities across Canada. An example of this is the recent emergence of the Canadian CLT Network that is fostering regular communication among CLT organizations across the country.

THE FIRST GENERATION OF CANADIAN CLTs
1980s–2012

A defining characteristic of this first cluster of largely sector-based CLTs,[3] which emerged from the 1980s to 2012, was the primary focus on the provision of cooperative and other forms of affordable housing through land ownership by the CLT organization. The emphasis on co-op housing provision derived from the strong Canadian cooperative housing movement that started in the 1930s (Hulchanski, 1988) and became a dominant affordable housing model in cities in the 1970s, with the development of well-regarded co-op housing projects such as St. Lawrence in Toronto and with the support of housing activists and municipal, provincial, and federal governments for this form of housing.

The CLT model, adopted through informal activist knowledge of the American CLT movement, became a conduit through which affordable housing, primarily co-op housing, was produced at a localized scale. We also observe a notable difference in the size and scope of CLTs during this period. Some CLTs, such as Colandco in Toronto and the Vernon District Community Land Trust in Vernon, British Columbia, adopted a sector-based and city-wide organizational approach with little community-led direction over the CLT organization itself. Conversely, other CLTs such as the West Broadway CLT embraced a more community-led, neighbourhood-based approach in the provision of affordable housing.

Colandco (Toronto)

The first two CLTs in Canada, both formed in the 1980s, focused on the provision of cooperative housing: Colandco in Toronto and Milton-Parc in Montreal. Colandco (initially called Inner City) was established in 1986 as a land holding and sector-based development company by the Co-operative Housing Federation of Toronto. Colandco purchased existing rental apartment buildings as well as parcels of land for the purpose of developing new multi-unit residential projects. Colandco retained ownership of the land and the buildings, while executing a 49-year lease with each cooperative for both. This arrangement provided the co-ops with use of the properties for the term of the lease. By retaining long-term ownership and control of the land and buildings, Colandco could ensure that the housing would remain affordable in perpetuity (Communitas Inc. 1985; Hulchanski, 1983; Interview with Tom Clement, February 18, 2019).

Colandco successfully leveraged its initial $2 million (CAD) of seed funding to develop an initial project,[4] the City Park Co-op, that secured 770 cooperative housing units through the acquisition of a privately owned rental project that was in receivership. Using the revolving fund as a deposit to secure the site, Colandco was subsequently able to mobilize funding and financing from the provincial government to complete the $63 million purchase. By the early 1990s, Colandco had assembled land ownership on a large scale for the development of fourteen housing cooperatives, containing a total of 2,350 housing units scattered across central Toronto, Scarborough, and Oshawa (Canada Mortgage and Housing Corporation, 2005; Co-operative Housing Federation of Toronto, 2019).

Colandco's program of land expansion and residential development started to face challenges in 1994, however, as a result of a global financial recession that began in the early 1990s and was significantly felt for several years in the province of Ontario. The withdrawal of governmental support for social housing and other affordable housing programs during the same period also impacted Colandco's projects. These pressures caused Colandco to downsize its housing development activities and to focus increasingly on retaining land ownership through a land trust arrangement with individual co-operatives (Canada Mortgage and Housing Corporation, 2005; Hulchanski 1983). Colandco entered into contractual agreements with individual nonprofit housing cooperatives to operate housing on its land, an approach that has had significant success and longevity in Toronto.

In 2017, Colandco and the Co-operative Housing Federation of Toronto took the lead in forming the Co-op Housing Land Trusts, consisting of four different land trusts: Colandco; the Bathurst Quay Co-op; Colandco's City Park Co-op; the Naismith Non-Profit Land Trust; and the Tenants Non-Profit Redevelopment Foundation (TNRC). These land trusts operate as a group. With the exception of the Bathurst Quay Co-op, each land trust has the same Board of Directors. Importantly, each land trust owns the land that is occupied by its cooperatives. As the leasee, each co-op is responsible for the management of its buildings. At the end of the land lease, the buildings will be transferred to the land trust unless the lease is renewed.

As a whole, the cooperatives that constitute the Co-op Housing Land Trusts are made up of thirty-two buildings, containing a total of 4,196 apartments or houses that are occupied by approximately 10,000 residents (Correspondence with Tom Clement, 2019). It is important to note that co-op residents are not organizational members of the Co-op Housing Land Trusts, but remain members of their individual cooperatives. This arrangement points to an innovative utilization of the community land trust model, where particular aspects of the CLT, such as land ownership and ground lease agreements, are combined with the autonomy of the co-op buildings. Resident members govern their individual cooperatives, but they may or may not have any involvement with the entity that owns the underlying land.

Communaute Milton-Parc (Montreal)

The Milton-Parc community, located in the downtown core of Montreal, has had similar success and longevity in the production of cooperative housing, while putting a creative, homegrown spin on the traditional CLT model. The idea for Communaute Milton-Parc (CMP) emerged from a lengthy resident-led and community-based struggle to save the neighbourhood from urban renewal plans proposed by a consortium of Montreal-based property developers. The activism of the Milton Parc Citizens Committee in the late 1960s and 1970s, which included street sit-ins and the occupation of buildings slated for demolition, succeeded in halting the renewal plans. The activists then formed multiple cooperative housing communities to purchase and to renovate the buildings, preserving this housing for low-income and middle-income residents (Kowaluk and Piche-Burton, 2012; Roussopoulos and Hawley, 2018).[5]

A growing concern about gentrification and displacement in the 1980s then led to the creation of the Communaute Milton-Parc in 1986. Approved by Quebec's provincial government, the CMP was viewed by the individual cooperatives as a way to protect housing affordability by protecting and stewarding the neighbourhood's land. Land titles in Milton-Parc are collectively owned by a syndicate of fifteen individual cooperatives and six nonprofit housing corporations through a Declaration of Co-Ownership. The CMP is governed by a general assembly constituted by the syndicate of co-owners. CMP acts as a governing and community decision-making body that regulates and sets guiding policy for cooperative ownership and community responsibility. CMP also owns and maintains the land beneath the common areas and enforces non-speculative restrictions on land uses and any land sales that might be contemplated by an individual cooperative (Ibid.).

Fig. 4.1. The Milton Parc neighbourhood, Montreal. OLIVIA WILLIAMS

CMP is an innovative take on the traditional structure of the CLT model. In the latter, the use of land and the affordability of housing are regulated through a ground lease for land that is owned by the CLT. Communaute Milton-Parc, by contrast, does not own the land beneath the housing itself but works as an overarching governance body for the Milton Parc neighbourhood that presently includes 148 buildings, 616 affordable units, and 1500 residents (Milton Parc, 2013). As a governance and decision-making body, the CMP arrangement offers a uniquely localized arrangement in which land is utilized and regulated in a way that best suits the preferences and circumstances of a particular neighbourhood. The organization has, over time, put in place a fulsome governance structure with a sophisticated assemblage of decision-making protocols and community engagement practices that connect the individual cooperatives and the overarching CMP body. This is combined with a focus on stopping residential displacement and supporting the longevity of affordable cooperative housing.

Milton Parc is the single largest cooperative housing neighbourhood in North America. Its size and success made Communaute Milton-Parc a finalist in the UN World Habitat Awards in 2013 (CMHC, 2005; World Habitat, 2017). Today, Milton Parc's residents remain active in public discussions about gentrification, displacement, and the need for affordable housing in Montreal. Importantly, they self-identify and publicly characterize their unique combination of fifteen cooperative housing communities, a single landholding syndicate, and an overarching structure of governance as being a community land trust.

CLT Formation in Central and Western Canada

In Colandco, the Co-op Housing Land Trusts, and Communaute Milton-Parc, we observe an emphasis on and support for long-term retention of affordable housing, whereby land trust arrangements serve as an innovative platform for producing and preserving housing that is cooperatively owned and managed. There was a similar focus on affordable housing provision among the community land trust organizations that arose in central and western Canada from the mid-1990s to mid-2000s. Without the existence of a formalized CLT network and, in most cases, without the existence of government legislation that would have legitimized or supported the existence of CLTs, such development tended to be ad hoc and localized.[6]

These CLTs were initiated by community activists who were searching for alternative, practical methods by which to attain affordable housing. They focused on individual homeownership, rather than cooperative housing, while working in partnership with private, for-profit developers and philanthropic affordable housing developers such as Habitat for Humanity. There is also evidence of informal knowledge sharing among these Canadian CLT organizers, who sometimes drew on personal information gathered about the implementation of the CLT model in the United States (Bunce, Khimani, *et al*, 2013).

West Broadway Community Land Trust (WBCLT) was the earliest example. It was established in 1999 as a subsidiary of the West Broadway Community Development Corporation (CMHC, 2005), located in the West Broadway neighbourhood of downtown Winnipeg, Manitoba. The community development corporation was a particularly innovative community development organization that focused on affordable housing and other social initiatives such as a community credit union, and was guided by concerns over local poverty issues caused by public disinvestment and encroaching gentrification/rising residential prices (Beaubien and Ring, 2006).

The intention of the WBCLT was to provide more diverse affordable housing tenure options in the form of rent-to-own homeownership, individual homeownership, cooperative homeownership, and affordable rental units (CMHC, 2005). A 2006 study of the WBCLT noted, however, that the primary focus of WBCLT was rent-to-own homeownership, addressing the needs of low-income households who were unable to move directly into homeownership but who might become homeowners over time with assistance (Beaubien and Ring, 2006). WBCLT assembled neighbourhood land parcels and purchased existing housing stock over a five-year period, offering a rent-to-own plan that was secured through a ground lease agreement between WBCLT and the tenant (who was also the potential owner).

This arrangement entailed the oversight of extensive renovations and the management of a complex array of funding from different governmental housing programs (Ibid., p. 3). Ultimately, WBCLT was unable to sustain the organizational and funding capacity that was needed both to undertake these renovations and to maintain the units through the duration of the rent-to-own period. This resulted in the eventual closure of the WBCLT as an arm of the West Broadway Community Development Corporation and the sale of some of its housing at market rate. Despite this failure, as Beaubien and Ring (Ibid.) noted, WBCLT played an important role in galvanizing community engagement and increasing public debate about land tenure as a component of community development, having a positive and lasting significance for the West Broadway community.

Other first-generation CLTs in central and western Canada faced similar challenges. The *Vernon and District Community Land Trust Society* (VDCLT) was formed in the province of British Columbia in 2008 to accrue public and philanthropic donations of lands and buildings for the development and management of affordable housing (Vernon and District Community Land Trust Society, 2012). The VDCLT's first project was a joint initiative with the City of Vernon, whereby the local government purchased land near the downtown core that was leased to the VDCLT through a long-term contractual arrangement and a small lease payment. The VDCLT, with Habitat for Humanity as a development partner, subsequently constructed rental units for low-income families and people with disabilities on this site. Since this initial project, the VDCLT has focused its efforts on accruing title to other lands and attaining public and philanthropic funding for additional affordable housing projects. It remains engaged with local communities in advocating for affordable housing in Vernon.

Also appearing in western Canada during this period was the *Calgary Community Land Trust* (CCLT). The CCLT was formed by the Calgary Homeless Foundation and was incorporated as a nonprofit organization in 2003 (Canada Mortgage and Housing Corporation, 2005). The CCLT focused on the assembly of land and building stock, as well as obtaining funds for the development and operation of affordable housing (Calgary Community Land Trust, 2012). CCLT received a donation of surplus federal government land, the result of a land swap between the federal government and the municipal government of Calgary, acquired for the purpose of building affordable housing on the land. The CCLT's first affordable housing project was the Sun Court development, completed in 2007, consisting of 27 units of owner-occupied family housing built by Habitat for Humanity Calgary (Calgary Homeless Foundation, 2012). The CCLT then went dormant for several years, as the work of the Calgary Homeless Foundation shifted towards more immediate and front-line initiatives to address homelessness in Calgary. It is now functioning as a CLT again, as we will discuss in the next section, reporting on more recent Canadian CLTs.

The *Central Edmonton Community Land Trust* (CECLT) emerged as a nonprofit corporation in 1998 with a mandate of fostering community-based development through land management and affordable housing provision. CECLT received donated land and properties from the municipal government of Edmonton and received funding from philanthropic foundations and development loans from the federal government's Canada Mortgage and Housing Corporation and Edmonton's Inner-City Housing Society. Unfortunately, due to difficulties in securing mortgages in the rent-to-own arrangements, CECLT had to repay Edmonton's government for the cost of the donated properties, selling them at market rate in order to raise reimbursement funds.

The situation in Edmonton highlights some of the broader challenges that were faced by the early CLTs in Canada, including: an inability to obtain mortgages for CLT home-owners; reliance on piecemeal and unpredictable government funding; and shifting political support for CLT activities from local government.

There were major differences among the CLTs that formed during this period, both in the tenure and scale of their projects and in the extent to which organizations and their activities were led by a place-based community. Some of these efforts, such as Milton-Parc and the West Broadway CLT, were community-led at the neighbourhood level, while the majority of CLTs during this period were driven by sector-based organizations such as the Co-operative Housing Federation of Canada (in the case of Colandco) and the Calgary Homeless Foundation (in the case of the Calgary Community Land Trust). Despite the small number of CLTs that emerged prior to 2012, however, they contributed to an emerging public awareness about the model's potential for delivering affordable housing (see Canada Mortgage and Housing Corporation, 2005). They also shaped a path for the formation of a second wave of CLT organizations.

THE SECOND GENERATION OF CANADIAN CLTs
2012–PRESENT

There has been a resurgence of interest in CLT development in Canada in recent years. Out of twenty currently active CLTs in Canada, nine were established since 2014. In 2017, moreover, a new Canadian CLT Network was formed to organize a more cohesive sector. This resurgence has been driven in part by the dynamic evolution of the small group of "first-generation," sector-based land trusts, which have re-emerged as expert-led nonprofit affordable housing developers. It also includes a new and energized "second generation" of more activist-based, community-based CLTs. The activists behind these latter initiatives — neighbourhood residents, community agencies, radical planners and, in some cases, municipal staff — have organized CLTs in response to the escalating affordable housing crisis in Canadian cities, rapid gentrification, and a renewed interest in community-based responses to these problems. While contemporary Canadian CLTs from both phases of CLT development share a common objective of increasing the supply of permanently affordable housing, they differ in their respective approaches to community-led development, community ownership, and democratic governance. We explore these issues in the following sections by referring to the activities of several representative second-generation CLTs.

Community-Based CLT Development

Since 2014, nine new community-led CLTs have emerged in response to an escalating affordable housing crisis in Canadian cities and a growing sense that government and social sector responses have been inadequate. This crisis, driven by an undersupply of housing, the increasing financialization of the housing market, and the repositioning by corporate landlords and private developers of existing housing for higher-income renters and homeowners, has translated into gentrification and redevelopment pressures in particular urban neighbourhoods (August and Walks, 2018; Bunce, 2018; Walks, 2014). For low-income and vulnerable residents, gentrification is a harmful process of destabilization. It causes food insecurity, housing insecurity, eviction, and displacement. While the social costs of gentrification are well known, neither the government nor the social housing sector has cultivated an adequate response. As a result, some impacted communities have looked to the community land trust as a way to mitigate gentrification.

The CLT model is appealing because of its emphasis on removing land and housing from the speculative market and controlling the rapid rise in real estate costs, thereby securing the perpetual affordability of land and housing. As Dominique Russell of the Kensington Market Land Trust in downtown Toronto's historic and gentrifying Kensington Market neighbourhood has stated, "Gentrification is a real estate problem and we felt we needed a real estate solution" (Interview with Dominique Russell, February 2, 2019, Toronto). Similar to first-generation CLTs, the current generation of community-led CLTs is focused on securing community ownership and/or community control of the land, whether through donation, purchase, or a long-term land lease from government, and then developing housing that will be permanently affordable. While CLT organizations retain ownership of the land, ownership of the building is retained by the CLT and leased to a nonprofit organization to provide affordable housing, or the building is owned directly by the nonprofit organization. Unlike sector-based CLTs, however, which view land ownership primarily as a legal tool to ensure affordable housing provision, the community-based organizations tend to have a broader agenda where community ownership of land is seen as the means to exercise broader community control over local development. They also engage in participatory democracy practices to fight against detrimental land uses and harmful real estate development decisions.

> The CLT is not only used for land preservation and housing provision, but also for planning and preserving socially just communities.

In urban areas like Toronto's Parkdale and Kensington Market neighbourhoods, Hamilton's Beasley neighbourhood, and the Heatherington area of Ottawa, where there is a long-standing working class, racialized, immigrant and socially progressive identity, gentrification threatens not only housing affordability, but collective social infrastructures, the local economy, and neighbourhood culture. In Vancouver's Hogan's Alley Society, the CLT acts as a way to redress the historical displacement of Vancouver's Black population. The CLT model provides a platform in such places for encouraging resident empowerment and participation and for exercising community control over neighbourhood change. In these contexts, the CLT is not only used for land preservation and housing provision, but also for planning and preserving more socially just communities.

Recent community-led CLTs have gone beyond a first-generation focus on the acquisition of land and the development of housing to engage more broadly in neighbourhood and city-wide activism, social rights advocacy, and community-led planning.

Parkdale Neighbourhood Land Trust (Toronto). The first of these second-generation, community-led CLTs to emerge was the Parkdale Neighbourhood Land Trust (PNLT). Established in 2014, the PNLT was initiated by residents and representatives from local nonprofit organizations who were concerned about the increasing gentrification of an historically working-class community. The intended role of the land trust was the acquisition and preservation of important community assets, removing them from the speculative market. A secondary goal was to enable increased democratic participation by neighbourhood residents in planning around land use. Although still in its start-up phase, PNLT has already generated strong local support. By mid 2019, it had attracted over 700 registered members and had completed two acquisitions, including an urban agricultural project and a rooming house preservation pilot project, which it intends to expand to build a portfolio of community-owned rooming houses.

Canada's charity law is more restrictive and burdensome than the 501(c)(3) designation in the United States. As a result, to accomplish its goals, Parkdale has developed a unique dual organizational model, consisting of a charity and a nonprofit that work together, but have different strategic purposes. The charitable land trust, called the Neighbourhood Land Trust (NLT), can benefit from charitable donations of land and money, but may only hold land that is used for charitable purposes and may only lease land to other charities. The charity cannot own cooperative housing or undertake community planning, both of which are not considered charitable purposes. It is also very limited in its ability to undertake political activity. The nonprofit land trust, the Parkdale Neighbourhood Land Trust (PNLT), has limited ability to fundraise, but can own and lease land more freely and has no limits on its political activity. The nonprofit land trust has a broad-based membership and community-elected board, while retaining control over the charity.

Inspired by CLTs in the United States, such as Dudley Neighbors Inc. in Boston and the Oakland CLT in the San Francisco Bay Area, PNLT has embraced the governance model of the "classic" CLT. Emphasizing community control of the organization itself, the PNLT's 15-person board of directors is elected from its resident membership. Furthermore, a tripartite board structure ensures equal representation from: "core members" who live or work on the trust's land; "organizational members" who are drawn from organizations that serve or embody the diversity of Parkdale; and "community members" who live or work within the geographic boundaries of Parkdale.

PNLT focuses its acquisition planning efforts on affordable housing and also space for community economic development, such as urban agriculture, social enterprises, and community services. With an interest in being responsive to community needs and

Fig. 4.2. PNLT members celebrating acquisition of at-risk rooming house, Toronto.

visions, the trust sets its priorities through community planning and action research. In 2016, PNLT co-led a participatory planning process, engaging 31 local organizations and over 400 residents in the creation of the *Parkdale Community Planning Study—A plan for decent work, shared wealth and equitable development in Parkdale*. The study identified an opportunity for the Neighborhood Land Trust to secure its first piece of land, a 7000 square-foot vacant property, which was acquired in 2017 through a below-market private purchase. The trust does not operate programs on the land it owns, but provides affordable land leases to eligible operating partners. Its first acquisition, now named the Milky Way Garden, is leased to Greenest City, a local environmental charity that will redevelop this vacant lot into an urban agriculture space to enhance affordable and equitable access to healthy food for local community members.

In 2017, the PNLT undertook a Community Action Research study of rooming house loss; a neighbourhood crisis that was quickly decreasing affordable single rooms and small rental units through the rapid conversion of rooming houses into upscaled rental housing or single-family homes. In response, the PNLT recruited four community organizations to implement a multi-partner Rooming House Preservation Strategy targeted to 59 at-risk rooming houses in Parkdale. Pursuing this strategy, after eight unsuccessful attempts, the Neighbourhood Land Trust has recently implemented a rooming housing preservation pilot, acquiring a 15-unit at-risk rooming house with capital funding provided by the City of Toronto. It is important to note that it was necessary to undertake two years of targeted advocacy and activism in order to build political support at the City of Toronto to make capital funding available to the land trust.[7] This funding enables and requires NLT to maintain rents at or below 80% of Average Market Rent (AMR) for a 99-year affordability period. Eligible tenants can also benefit from deeper levels of affordability, however, through rental supplements. The property will be held by the charitable NLT, but leased and operated by PARC, a local supportive housing organization.

The asset bases of PNLT and NLT are not large. Nevertheless, their public advocacy and higher profile in the press have contributed greatly to the growing public awareness and interest in CLTs, both in Toronto and across Canada.

Hamilton Community Land Trust (Ontario). The Hamilton Community Land Trust (HCLT) was formed in 2014 in the Beasley neighbourhood of Hamilton, Ontario by residents and community-based organizations who saw the need for greater community control over land use and the revitalization of Central Hamilton. This historically working-class city has long suffered from economic decline, environmental contamination, and high vacancy rates, but by 2014 a new phase of real estate reinvestment and gentrification was well underway. Between 2012 and 2015, housing prices in Hamilton rose significantly. HCLT's mandate is to hold and to steward land, acquired primarily from the municipality, and to facilitate the land's use for affordable housing or other community needs. The CLT is playing a facilitative role in the development of its lands, rather than that of a developer or operator, by working with resident groups, housing developers, and other organizations to transform underutilized properties into high-quality affordable housing, gardens, and community spaces. In 2017, HCLT acquired its first parcel of land from the City of Hamilton and then partnered with Habitat for Humanity Hamilton to develop a four-bedroom home that is being leased to a lower-income family. This initial project has demonstrated the capacity of HCLT to act as a viable organizational vehicle for redeveloping vacant city land (Hamilton Community Land Trust, 2019).

Kensington Market Community Land Trust (Toronto). Kensington Market Community Land Trust (KMCLT) was initiated in 2017 by an activist-minded group of residents who had successfully mobilized to stop the development of a WalMart store near an entrance road to the neighbourhood. The group aims to utilize the CLT to protect neighbourhood affordability more generally. Dominique Russell of KMCLT states that, "The fundamental underpinning characteristic of Kensington Market is its affordability, and we want to ensure this is preserved into the future" (Russell Interview, 2019). In recent years, Kensington Market has experienced increasing condominium development around the edges of the neighbourhood, rising rents, and "renovictions" linked to a surge in residential rehabilitation and the proliferation of short-term rentals such as AirBnB in the area. For long-term tenants and small independent store owners in this historically immigrant community, there is a shared interest in finding a way to remain in the neighbourhood and to protect its unique character (Ibid.).

KMCLT is planning to utilize the CLT for community ownership of land and community control over whatever is built upon it. The organization hopes to acquire and to preserve at-risk rental housing and storefronts. Potentially it may also oversee the redevelopment of a large municipal parking lot into a new affordable housing building. While KMCLT is still in its start-up phase of CLT development, its early success has generated support from local residents and representatives of the municipal government.

Hogan's Alley Society (Vancouver). Fifty years ago, after decades of displacement pressure on the community, the construction of the Georgia and Dunsmuir viaducts displaced an area historically known as Hogan's Alley, home to the city's Black population (Hogan's Alley Society, n.d.). In recent years, the City of Vancouver has focused efforts on removing the viaducts and is planning to revitalize the area through the North East False Creek (NEFC) area plan, approved in 2018. The Hogan's Alley Society was formed as a community-led nonprofit organization in 2017 to seek redress for the displacement of the Black community by fostering social, political, cultural and economic justice for Vancouver's Black community. Through a proposal for a nonprofit community land trust, the Hogan's Alley Society seeks to steward the land and to oversee the development of affordable housing, cultural amenities, social enterprise, and small business spaces, managing these assets in perpetuity. Negotiations with the City of Vancouver are also underway for a transfer of the former Hogan's Alley site into the CLT, a commitment made in the NEFC policy by the City Council in 2018. The redevelopment and stewardship of these lands will be led by the Hogan's Alley Society, working with partners and stakeholders in applying the CLT model to support renter households (Hogan's Alley Society, n.d.).

Sector-Based Community Land Trusts

While community-led CLTs have generated new interest in the CLT as a model for bottom-up development, sector-based CLTs have continued to demonstrate that the CLT is an effective vehicle for the development and stewardship of large stocks of affordable housing. Some first-generation CLTs, such as Colandco, have halted their housing development activities and now focus purely on the stewardship of their assets. Others are forging new growth plans. The recent formation of the Vancouver Community Land Trust Foundation (VCLTF) and HomeSpace (formerly the Calgary Community Land Trust) underscore a new phase of sector-based CLT development led by organizations with expansionist business approaches. As a result, these two sector-based CLTs are building thousands of units of new affordable housing on community-owned land and, in the process, are creating broader public recognition of the CLT model in Canada.

The Community Land Trust (Vancouver). The most prolific sector-based CLT development to be undertaken in the past decade has been led by the Cooperative Housing Federation of British Columbia (CHFBC), which controls three CLTs in the wider Vancouver area, collectively branded as *The Community Land Trust*. This recent development has occurred in the context of Vancouver's expensive housing market which, in turn, has sparked a renewed interest in cooperative and nonprofit affordable housing provision. The success of the three Vancouver-area land trusts was facilitated by enabling policy and political will at both the provincial and municipal levels. In this light, the CHFBC has imagined the CLT as a development and asset management vehicle that can deliver and steward affordable housing in direct partnership with government and the broader community housing sector.

Following in the footsteps of Colandco in Toronto, CHFBC created the Community Housing Land Trust Foundation in 1993 to hold the land and buildings of multiple cooperatives. In its early years, the Foundation acquired six properties, containing 354 units, transferred from the provincial government. The Foundation retained ownership of the land and the buildings, executing leases for the land and buildings with the independent housing cooperatives.

In 2012, a unique opportunity emerged for the CHFBC to establish a second land trust, the Vancouver Community Land Trust Foundation (VCLTF), when it won a bid competition to develop four parcels of land that were owned by the City of Vancouver. That year, CHFBC re-envisioned its model and began to self-identify as a community land trust, even rebranding its multiple land trust efforts as "The Community Land Trust." This re-framing was partially political: emphasizing the nonprofit ownership and stewardship of the land and buildings in contrast to the private provision of affordable housing that was being proposed by other developers who were competing for access to public land. It also signaled that the CLT would serve the broader community housing sector, including nonprofit and Indigenous organizations, rather than serving only cooperatives.

VCLTF has since successfully developed 358 affordable housing units on these four parcels of land. While title to the land has been retained by the City of Vancouver, the CLT has a 99-year leasehold for the land and owns the buildings until the end of the lease, when all of the improvements will revert to the City. VCLTF hopes that, at the end of this lease period, the CLT and the City will work together to redevelop the property for purposes that are consistent with their respective missions (Interview with Tom Armstrong, July 21, 2019).

Three of these properties are owned by the Community Land Trust and operated as rental housing, managed through operating agreements with three different nonprofit housing organizations. The fourth property is operated by a housing cooperative. Since the housing is operated by other organizations, the VCLTF is free to focus on other

> The Vancouver CLT Foundation has become a preferred partner for doing residential development on municipally owned land.

aspects of development and stewardship. Across its entire portfolio, tenants pay rents that range from a shelter rate to 90% of Average Market Rent. Building on this successful partnership with the City of Vancouver, VCLTF won another competitive bid in 2018 to develop an additional 1000 new affordable rental units on seven parcels of City-owned land.

While CLTs in Canada have historically faced challenges in increasing their scale, VCLTF has addressed this issue by forging strong partnerships with municipalities and by maximizing the benefits of a portfolio approach to development and stewardship; that is, when planning for new developments, VCLTF utilizes revenues generated from more profitable properties to cross-subsidize less profitable properties. This has allowed VCLTF to develop properties which may not have otherwise been financially viable. VCLTF's ability to develop affordable housing on a wide range of properties has positioned it as a preferred partner by the City of Vancouver for doing residential development on municipally owned land.

Significantly, through its multiple land trusts, CHFBC has departed from the standard practice of CLTs in other countries and has occasionally chosen to encumber its landholdings with debt, thereby "unlocking" the equity to leverage the financing needed for the development of new affordable housing. As Tiffany Duzzita, VCLTF's Director, notes:

> [T]he community land trust is a vehicle for keeping the affordable housing sector growing, and it comes down to benefits derived from the separation of land and buildings. The land component stays with the land trust, removing it from the speculative market and rising real estate costs. But the nonprofit land trust can actually use the land value as equity to redevelop and build new housing by borrowing against it. Since the land trust is mission based—it uses its (growing equity) to build more housing, not generate profit (Presentation by Tiffany Duzzita, 2017).

The community land trust has also proven to be a successful conduit through which to stabilize, improve, and redevelop existing cooperative housing assets. Recently, VCLTF took ownership of 94 cooperative homes in Abbotsford BC after the co-op experienced financial challenges. VCLTF worked with co-op members to design a comprehensive renovation plan that was funded through refinancing their existing mortgages. By bringing the co-op's assets into the land trust, the co-op benefited from an increased asset management capacity. Additionally, VCLTF provided a guarantee that the land would be protected for affordable housing on a long-term basis. Tiffany Duzzita estimates that in twelve years, the land trust will be able to leverage the increased value in the land to fund the development of an estimated 200 new units of affordable housing at the Abbotsford site, requiring little to no government assistance (Presentation by Duzzita, 2017).

HomeSpace (Calgary). The initial vision for Calgary's HomeSpace, in its previous incarnation as the Calgary Community Land Trust, was to focus on receiving cash and land donations for affordable housing, but not to develop or to operate the housing itself. HomeSpace now identifies as a nonprofit real estate corporation that seeks to provide development, property management, and asset management capacity to the affordable housing sector through the land trust model. As of early 2019, HomeSpace owned 27 buildings with a total of 520 rental units, and had an additional 211 units under development. Utilizing a partnership model, HomeSpace retains ownership of the buildings it develops and provides property management, while 17 agency partners provide support services to residents with the intention of serving diverse populations. Rents are offered at a "break-even" rate that is 20%–40% below market, with many tenants receiving deeper levels of affordability through housing allowances. One characteristic that sets Home-Space apart from many other CLTs is that it explicitly focuses on developing properties for supportive housing. It is also distinctive in not separating the ownership of land and buildings. HomeSpace continues to own both.

Over several years, HomeSpace has increased its capacity to become one of the largest nonprofit housing developers in Calgary. In 2018, HomeSpace won competitive bids to build affordable housing on three parcels of land that were owned by the City of Calgary. HomeSpace attributes its recent success and growth in part to the high level of coordination of affordable housing efforts in Calgary. The Calgary Homeless Foundation acts as the systems planner, working with local agencies and government to identify areas of greatest need, while HomeSpace acts as the nonprofit developer in partnership with government and specialized housing providers to develop projects and to serve as their long-term steward after they are built (HomeSpace Society, 2018).

CANADIAN NETWORK OF CLTs

There are currently twenty active CLTs in Canada, half of which were initiated since 2014. This recent surge in CLT development in Canada coalesced in July 2017 with the establishment of the Canadian Network of CLTs (CNCLT).[8] This new Network aims to unite both newer, community-led CLTs and more established CLTs into a cohesive, nation-wide movement. Initial objectives of the Canadian Network of CLTs include: (1) increasing government recognition of the CLT model through legislative advocacy; (2) increasing peer-to-peer resource sharing and capacity building; and (3) centering of social justice in CLT development.

In 2019, over 30 members of the fledgling Network met in person in Canada for the first time at a conference hosted by Communaute Milton-Parc in Montreal, entitled *From The Ground Up: Community Control of Land, Housing and the Economy.*

The Canadian CLT Network (*www.communityland.ca*) is still new and remains fairly ad hoc in its organization, but it has already increased collaboration and resource sharing among Canadian CLTs. If the Network can successfully facilitate cross-pollination and capacity building between community-led approaches and sector-based CLT approaches, the expectation is that Canadian CLTs will continue to grow as necessary structures for more socially just planning and affordable housing provision, while also having a greater impact on public policies.

﹀

CONCLUSION

The recent growth of CLTs in Canada builds upon several decades of organizing, from the 1980s onwards. In the context of large-scale government cutbacks in funding for social housing programs, social services, and community programs over the past several decades, Canadian CLTs have emerged as a relatively small, yet effective vehicle for meeting community needs and broader public priorities for affordable housing.

The "first generation" of CLTs that emerged in the 1980s were either large, sector-based organizations that prioritized affordable housing provision across cities and urban regions through partnerships with co-op housing societies, or neighbourhood-oriented and focused on community-based development through local affordable housing provision. This difference is evident in the organizational development of Colandco over the past several decades and its use of a land trust arrangement to include a portfolio of individual cooperative housing communities across Toronto. In contrast, the West Broadway CLT in Winnipeg chose to remain neighbourhood-focused, concentrating on the renovation of rent-to-own housing and supporting local community development efforts. Several of the CLTs in this first phase of Canadian CLT development created their own variations on the American CLT model, informed by the Canadian adoption of cooperatives, as a way to create affordable communities.

After 2012, the emergence of a "second generation" of CLTs followed a similar pattern of being either sector-based and expansionist in their approach to affordable housing provision or community-led and neighbourhood-based. The growth of CLTs during this period, especially over the last several years, has reflected the influence of local activists advocating for the particular needs of their surrounding community. This is evident in CLT initiatives that more broadly address the impact of gentrification, such as in Parkdale, Hamilton, and Hogan's Alley. Sector-led CLTs, on the other hand, such as the Vancouver Community Land Trust and HomeSpace, demonstrate innovative strategies to accrue land and to act as affordable housing developers through the formation of multi-sectoral partnerships and sophisticated management of their housing portfolios. With a city-wide service area, these sector-based CLTs are expanding affordable housing supply and, at the same time, increasing public awareness about the potential productivity and viability of the CLT model.

The recent establishment of a Canadian Network of CLTs, bringing together sector-based and community-based CLTs in a formal network for resource sharing and knowledge mobilization, points to a new phase of CLT development in Canada. CLT organizations are now actively engaged in creating links with one another and with organizations and networks in other countries. There has also been, of late, a much-needed discussion about Indigenous land rights and national reconciliation in relation to CLTs. Building on several decades of organizational development and advocacy, Canadian CLTs are now creating a new wave of innovative practices and opportunities for affordable housing provision and community-led development.

Notes

1. A National Housing Strategy for Canada, the first federal government initiative for affordable housing in several decades, was announced by the Liberal government in their 2016 budget. This Strategy is a 10-year, $40 billion plan to address homelessness and to subsidize the production of 100,000 new affordable housing units (National Housing Strategy, 2018).

2. 96% of all housing in Canada is currently built by the private sector (Cheung, 2017).

3. Throughout this chapter we use the term "sector-based" to refer to the nonprofit housing sector. This is a common colloquial term used by affordable housing advocates in Canada.

4. This $2 million seed grant was provided by the Campeau Corporation, a Canadan-based commercial and residential real estate development firm (Canada Mortgage and Housing Corporation, 2005).

5. The renovation of these buildings and other infrastructure was publicly funded at an estimated cost of $30 million (CAD), provided by the Canadian Mortgage and Housing Corporation, the City of Montreal, and the provincial government of Quebec (World Habitat, 2017).

6. In Canada, legislation for local level (municipal) governance is produced and enacted by provincial or territorial governments. There are ten provincial governments and three territorial governments.

7. Because of this project, the City of Toronto piloted a new approach to distributing capital funding through a fast-tracked approval process that enabled PNLT to act quickly to acquire the property on the open market.

8. The first meetings were held online with support from Grounded Solutions Network in the United States. They included representatives from Parkdale Neighbourhood Land Trust, Kensington Market CLT, Circle CLT, Colandco, Hamilton CLT, Vivacité (Montreal), Hogan's Alley, Communaute Milton-Parc, Vancouver's Community Land Trust, the North End Halifax CLT (Nova Scotia), and Heatherington Land Trust (Ottawa).

References

August, M. & Walks, A. (2018). "Gentrification, Suburban Decline, and the Financialization of Multi-Family Rental Housing: The Case of Toronto." *Geoforum* 89, 124–136.

Beaubien, LA. & Ring, L. (2006). *Preserving Community: Examining the West Broadway Community Land Trust.* Unpublished report.

Bunce, S. (2018). *Sustainability Policy, Planning, and Gentrification in Cities.* Routledge, Abingdon.

Bunce, S., Khimani, N., Sungu-Erylimaz, Y., and Earle, E. (2013). *Urban Community Land Trusts: Experiences from Canada, the United States, and Britain.* University of Toronto, Toronto.

Calgary Homeless Foundation (2012). *Calgary Homeless Foundation 2012 Annual Report.* Calgary Homeless Foundation, Calgary.

Canada Mortgage and Housing Corporation (2005). *Critical Success Factors for Community Land Trusts in Canada: Final Report.* Canada Mortgage and Housing Corporation, Ottawa.

Canadian Cooperative Housing Federation of Toronto (2019) *<https://co-ophousingtoronto.coop>* Last accessed: July 1, 2019.

Communitas Inc. (1985). *Land Trusts for Non-Profit Continuing Housing Co-operatives.* Cooperative Housing Federation of Canada.

Hamilton Community Land Trust (2019). *<https://www.hamiltonclt.org>* Last accessed: July 22, 2019.

Home Space Society (2018). *<https://www.homespace.org>* Last accessed: July 22, 2019.

Hogan's Alley Society (n.d.). *<http://www.hogansalleysociety.org>* Last accessed: July 22, 2019.

Hulchanski, D. (1983). "Co-operative Land Management: The Potential of Linking a Community Land Trust to Government Housing Supply Programs," Pp. 35–50 in: D. Hulchanski (Ed.) *Managing Land for Housing: The Experience of Housing Co-operatives in British Columbia.* Centre for Human Settlements, University of British Columbia.

Hulchanski, D. (1988). "The Evolution of Property Rights and Housing Tenure in Post-War Canada: Implications for Housing Policy," *Urban Law and Policy* 9, 135–156.

Interview with Brian Finley (2013). Toronto.

Interview with Tom Clement (2019). Toronto.

Interview with Dominique Russell (2019). Toronto.

Interview with Tom Armstrong (2019). Toronto.

Kowaluk, L. & Piche-Burton, C. (eds.)(2012). *Communaute Milton-Parc: How We Did It and How It Works Now.* Communaute Milton-Parc, Montreal.

La Communaute Milton Parc (2013). <*http://www.miltonparc.org/about-us/*> Last accessed: July 22, 2019.

Presentation by Tiffany Duzzita (2017). ONPHA Conference, Niagara Falls.

Roussopoulos, Dimitrios and Hawley, Josh (eds.)(2018). *Villages in Cities: Community Land Ownership, Cooperative Housing, and the Milton Parc Story.* Montreal: Black Rose Books.

Vernon and District Community Land Trust Society (2012). <*http://www.communityland. ca/canadian-clts/*> Last accessed: July 22, 2019.

Walks, A. (2014). "From Financialization to Socio-Spatial Polarization of the City: Evidence from Canada," *Economic Geography* 90(1), 33–66.

World Habitat (2017). Milton Parc Community <*https://www.world-habitat.org/world-habitat-awards/winners-and-finalists/milton-park-community/*> Last accessed: July 22, 2019.

5.

Seeding the CLT in Latin America and the Caribbean
Origins, Achievements, and the Proof-of-Concept Example of the Caño Martín Peña Community Land Trust

María E. Hernández-Torrales, Lyvia Rodríguez Del Valle, Line Algoed, and Karla Torres Sueiro

The Fideicomiso de la Tierra del Caño Martín Peña (Caño CLT) is a community land trust designed and controlled by the residents of seven neighborhoods along the Martín Peña Channel, a highly polluted tidal estuary that runs through the heart of San Juan, the capital of Puerto Rico. The Caño CLT was created with the aim to regularize land tenure and to prevent involuntary displacement and gentrification, precipitated by the government's planned dredging and clean-up of the channel. Creation of the Caño CLT and the channel's ecological restoration are among the main elements of the wider ENLACE Caño Martín Peña Project. This initiative has brought together community residents and partners from the private and public sectors to implement a comprehensive development plan designed to uplift a historically marginalized area, while transforming this urban area into a more habitable, just and participatory space.

Residents of seven Martín Peña neighborhoods[1] adopted the community land trust (CLT), but adapted it to meet local needs. By adding completely new elements to the model and by applying it to address the problem of land insecurity in an informal settlement, the Caño CLT has become an important reference world-wide, specifically in the Global South. Roughly 1,500 very low- to moderate-income households are now members of the Caño CLT, which currently owns and manages more than 110 hectares (272 acres) of land, most of which previously belonged to governmental agencies. The Caño CLT ensures the availability of permanently affordable housing and provides alternative housing options on its land for families who have had to relocate because of the dredging of the channel. It is also an instrument for the generation and redistribution of wealth.

The Fideicomiso de la Tierra del Caño Martín Peña is one of three institutions that resulted from a broad participatory planning-action-reflection process that took place between 2002 and 2004. During the planning process, twelve community-based organizations from the Martín Peña communities came together as a collective in the Group of the Eight Communities Adjacent to the Caño Martín Peña, Inc. (G-8). In collaboration with external partners from Puerto Rico's private and public universities and other professional and technical allies, they drafted regulatory instruments such as the Comprehensive Development and Land Use Plan for the Special Planning District of the Caño Martín Peña (the District Plan) and Law 489 of September 24, 2004 for the Comprehensive Development of the Special Planning District of the Caño Martín Peña (Law 489-2004). Through this law, not only the Caño CLT was created, but also a government corporation, the ENLACE Project Corporation, charged with responsibility for implementing the District Plan with a prominent role of the residents.

Initially conceived to regularize land tenure, to facilitate the implementation of the District Plan and to guarantee access of these consolidated communities to urban land whose value was increasing, the Caño CLT is continuing its work in the midst of a double crisis. Puerto Rico has been struggling with financial distress and an unpayable public debt since 2006. Then, two devastating hurricanes hit the island in September 2017.[2] Puerto Rico has become one of the only places in the world that is simultaneously going through the contradictory processes of both austerity and recovery, while exhibiting the designs and dangers of what is known as "disaster capitalism" (Bonilla & LeBron, 2019; Algoed & Hernández, 2019).

Puerto Rico is an unincorporated territory of the United States, a result of the Cuban-Spanish-American War when the United States installed colonial governments in the Philippines, Guam and Puerto Rico. Today, Puerto Rico and Guam continue to be under U.S. sovereignty. According to the U.S. Census Bureau, in 2018 Puerto Rico had a population of 3.2 million. Since the start of the financial crisis, however, half-a-million Puerto Ricans have left the island. Another 160,000 emigrated to the United States after Hurricane María.[3] When the Caño CLT was created, the main threats faced by the communities along the channel were involuntary displacement and gentrification, a result of an increase in the value of the area's land. Today, the main threat comes from a decrease in value which, in combination with the government's current austerity and disaster recovery policies, have created conditions favorable to speculation. Under both cycles of increasing and decreasing land value, the Caño CLT has proven to be an effective instrument to protect the community against displacement.

This chapter discusses how the Caño CLT is facilitating the regularization of land tenure in seven informal settlements, while preventing gentrification and furthering implementation of the District Plan. Inhabitants of this area transformed an infrastructure project that was initially led by the government into a participatory project of comprehensive development, one that is working to overcome historical causes of poverty, while also restructuring the government's relationship with the marginalized communities within this special planning district. Together with their external partners, the Caño residents have created a viable CLT that aims to protect their right to land, their right to adequate housing, their right to live in the city with dignity, their right to health, and their right to participate in the decisions that affect their future, including those related to the use and development of their land. The components of this project combine to counteract the way in which a lack of community participation in large-scale infrastructure projects normally leads to forced displacement and structural urban inequality.

The ability of G-8, ENLACE, and the Fideicomiso de la Tierra to unite people toward a common cause in a deeply divisive context has been recognized internationally. Since winning the United Nations World Habitat Award in 2016, the Caño CLT has become an example and an inspiration for activists around the world who are working on land tenure issues and looking for an alternative form of land regularization. One of only two community land trusts in the world that have been organized in an informal settlement,[4] the Caño CLT has become a touchstone for communities in the Global South in particular, who are looking to establish CLTs of their own to overcome the threat of displacement from lands strategically located in desirable areas.

The chapter is organized into four sections. First, we present a historical overview and political context to help the reader to understand that, although Puerto Rico is part of the United States, the multiple obstacles faced by the Martín Peña communities are both enormous and exceptional. Then, we describe how the Caño CLT was created and why the communities opted for a CLT to address their needs. After explaining how the CLT functions, we reflect on the importance of the Fideicomiso as a reference for other communities that are struggling with similar threats of displacement from their land and why they might look to the Caño CLT for inspiration.

I. LAND, DISPLACEMENT AND INFORMAL SETTLEMENTS IN PUERTO RICO

The relationship with the land has always been a subject of struggle in Puerto Rico. As in the rest of Latin America, the history of Puerto Rico is defined by colonialism and the repeated displacement of vulnerable populations. A colony of the United States since 1898, the Caribbean island lacks economic sovereignty. Decades of dependence and tax exemptions aimed at attracting and extracting wealth have put major stresses on the island's economy. With a current unaudited public debt of over $74 billion, the Commonwealth of Puerto Rico was forced to apply austerity measures, imposed by the Fiscal Oversight Board created under PROMESA (Puerto Rico Oversight, Management and Economic Stability Act). This law, adopted by the U.S. Congress in 2016 during the Obama presidency, created the Fiscal Oversight Board to guarantee payments to bondholders, most

> Little by little, control of the island's land has moved to those who do not use it for the benefit of the country.

of them speculators. Public employees and retirees have been seeing their salaries and pensions jeopardized, approximately 280 schools have been closed, and the budget of the public university has been drastically reduced. Insecurity due to the cuts, the high unemployment rate, and the high cost of living have made life on the island challenging for a large part of its population.

This economic crisis is the result of the expiration of federal tax exemptions for United States companies, which had previously turned the island into one of the more attractive places to locate for North American companies. The growth of the economy depended on these tax exemptions. When these tax exemptions expired in 2006, most of the companies abandoned Puerto Rico, leaving thousands of highly skilled Puerto Ricans unemployed. There has been virtually no economic growth since then.

Land is one of the only assets that the government can still monetize. Tax incentives that took place after 2012 have attracted investors to the island to buy land to develop luxury complexes. Little by little, control of the island's land has moved to those who do not use it for the benefit of the country, during a period when it has become increasingly difficult for Puerto Ricans to find employment, to buy land, or to pay off their mortgage loans. Disaster recovery and other policies adopted after Hurricanes Irma and María have exacerbated the situation. Puerto Rico is almost fully under the Opportunity Zones program, which provides generous U.S. federal tax exemptions to investors and is particularly attractive for the real estate sector. Meanwhile, the Action Plan[5] prepared by Puerto Rico and approved by the U.S. Department of Housing and Urban Development has a series of policies that promote the displacement of communities in high-risk areas, even when mitigation is feasible. Concurrently, the government permits privately funded reconstruction and developments in similar high-risk areas.

Investing in luxury properties in depressed sectors — which, in the case of Puerto Rico, includes most of the island — can result in increases in the land values, contributing to the displacement of low-income and moderate-income residents. The displacement of poor communities can, in turn, lead to further increases in land values (Navas, 2004: 4).

According to the government Office for Socio-Economic and Community Development, there are 742 communities across Puerto Rico that have been categorized as informal settlements. The rapid industrialization of the island in the 1930s and 1940s, which made Puerto Rico an example of "advanced capitalism," pushed impoverished peasants into the coastal cities in search of employment and health and education services for their children. As affordable housing was not available, they occupied land that was unsuitable for housing, such as mangroves, wetlands, steep mountain slopes, and areas very close to the sea. Many of these families settled in the wetlands along the Martín Peña Channel, at the outskirts of San Juan, building makeshift homes on stilts with cardboard, coconut trees, wood, and tin. They used wooden planks to create connections among the homes

Fig. 5.1. Aerial view of neighborhoods surrounding the Martín Peña Channel (top), and a house alongside the Martín Peña Channel. LINE ALGOED / J.E. DAVIS

and to have access to the dry land and roads. With time, the families and the Municipality of San Juan filled the wetlands with debris.

Today, almost 25,000 people still live in eight neighborhoods along the channel. As the city grew, their location became prime real estate next to the financial district and along the channel that, once dredged, will serve as an inland waterway connecting the main airport with tourist-oriented hubs. The once-navigable channel is clogged and heavily polluted, as most neighborhoods lack an adequate sewage system and functioning storm-water management systems.

Between the 1960s and 1980s, as development policies were aimed at eliminating "slums," several communities along the western half of the Caño were relocated to

Fig. 5.2. One of the Caño's major streets, looking toward San Juan's financial district (top) and a side street in a Caño neighborhood. DOEL VÁZQUEZ / J.E. DAVIS

public housing or evicted. There were various proposals to recover the Caño area either for conservation purposes, for highways or for high-end developments including hotels and marinas. Most of these plans called for the displacement of remaining Martín Peña communities. Relocation costs were not even considered, and neither was community participation (Algoed, Hernández and Rodríguez, 2018). With the establishment of the financial district and the advancement of individual land-titling programs, gentrification became a new threat. Speculators started buying those individually owned plots of land, particularly those closest to the main transportation corridors, knowing that the possible ecosystem restoration of the channel would drastically increase the value of the area's land. These threats, coupled with the announcement in 2002 that the government was going to pursue the dredging of the channel, would become the issues around which the residents of the Martín Peña communities organized to find a solution for their common problems.

II. CREATION OF THE CAÑO MARTÍN PEÑA CLT

Public participation in the planning process for government-sponsored projects that affect residential areas has rarely happened in Puerto Rico. That remained the pattern even after the Puerto Rico Planning Board was mandated by law to open the planning processes to comments and participation by the public. This started to change under the administration of Governor Sila M. Calderón. In March 2001, the Governor signed the first statute of her new administration, proclaiming as a public policy the empowerment of residents of low-income communities (Law 1, March 1, 2001). This public policy encouraged citizen partic-ipation, defined as a comprehensive process enabling citizens to recognize and to exercise full control of their lives, starting from their own efforts and power. According to the Law, such an initiative would be aimed at helping the residents of low-income communities to acquire the skills and levels of organization that might allow them to become authors of their own process of economic and social development. The government would act as a train-er, promoter, facilitator, and collaborator, eliminating barriers and creating the necessary conditions and mechanisms to enable communities to secure their personal and commu-nity development. Governmental agencies and instrumentalities were required to carry out well-planned actions to stimulate the participation of low-income communities in the deci-sion-making processes related to the issues affecting their development. These communities would assume new roles as owners and producers, implementing a participatory approach to planning and improving their neighborhoods, which was radically different from the past practice of being passive beneficiaries of a paternalistic state. This public policy enabled the participatory approach that was used in the ENLACE Project.

From an Infrastructure Project
to a Sustainable Development Project

Instead of hiring engineers, the Authority hired an urban planner to lead the effort and estab-lished a Community Participation Office in a trailer located at the heart of the Caño com-munities, and staffed with community social workers and organizers. The Authority also pursued the establishment, by the Puerto Rico Planning Board, of the Caño Martin Peña Special Planning District, comprised by seven of the eight communities[6] remaining along the tidal channel. Residents participated in high numbers during the first round of commu-nity assemblies as they learned about the plans to dredge the channel, and strongly voiced their concern around displacement. They questioned where the families living close to the channel would be taken, as the space was needed for the dredging. Moreover, and conscious of the strategic location of their neighborhoods, they questioned who would benefit from the project, and clearly expressed their intent to oppose any attempt to gentrify. The meeting

Fig. 5.3. Election of new community council for Comunidad Las Monjas, one of the Caño's G-8 communities. LINE ALGOED

sparked one of the most successful participatory community development processes in Puerto Rico's history.

From 2002 to 2004, more than 700 participatory planning, action, and reflection activities were held in the Martín Peña communities. Concurrently, residents were envisioning the future and designing strategies, implementing projects and programs for short-term wins addressing their pressing issues, while organizing and critically thinking and learning about the process that was being implemented. The residents received the information they needed to participate intelligently in drafting the development plan, and technical consultants engaged in a dialogue that valued the knowledge of the residents rather than downplaying it. Had residents been left out of this process, the plan would have been inadequate and incomplete. The end result was the *Comprehensive Development and Land Use Plan for the Caño Martín Peña Special Planning District* (Development Plan), which was officially adopted by the Puerto Rico Planning Board and approved by the Governor of Puerto Rico in 2007. The inclusive process that produced this Plan took what had started out as a typical top-down engineering project and turned it the participatory, equitable and sustainable community development initiative called the ENLACE Caño Martín Peña Project.

Today, there are approximately 120 community leaders active within the G-8, mostly women and youth; indeed, 40% are young leaders between the ages of 11–25 years old. Another 100 residents form a network with a person per-street who is tasked with keeping their neighbors informed of the activities that are taking place, as thirty different socio-economic, housing, and urban development initiatives are underway with residents playing an active role in each.

Development Without Displacement

The Development Plan assumed that the Martín Peña communities would gain control over the publicly owned land within the Caño Martín Peña Special Planning District. This would accomplish three important goals. First, land would become available for the housing and infrastructure projects necessary to improve the quality of life of the residents and to address constant flooding with polluted water. Taking the cost of land out of the equation, moreover, would lower the implementation costs and increase the project's feasibility in the context of Puerto Rico's dire financial and economic situation. Second, having control of the land would allow residents who were living in areas where land was needed to build infrastructure projects and to dredge the channel to be relocated within one of the Caño's neighborhoods, avoiding their involuntary displacement. Third, gentrification would be prevented. Community residents were aware that once the infrastructure project took place and the channel was dredged, the cost of land and housing within the Martín Peña area would soar and existing residents would surely and steadily be pushed aside. With this in mind, having control of the land would prevent the displacement of residents who lacked land titles by regularizing their relationship with the land and allowing them to have security of tenure.

> Residents were aware that once the channel was dredged, the cost of land would soar.

Land ownership was a central piece for the community to reach its goal, so choosing the right mechanism to regularize tenure was critical. Several strategies were used to provoke discussions around land tenure. To help with the anaylsis of tenure options, a Housing Committee was created, composed of representatives from the seven Caño neighborhoods in the Special Planning District.

A workshop was held where participants were asked to identify why families wanted to have individual titles to the land — the form of tenure with which people were most familiar. The common answers included: the desire of the residents to bequeath the right to occupy a parcel of land to their legal heirs; access to public services (i.e., safe connections to the power grid required a permit); and access to mortgage credit. All participants agreed that avoiding the displacement of the community was a priority. After learning from experts about the pros and cons of individual land titles, land coops, and community land trusts, participants were able to examine how each ownership instrument might allow them to reach their objectives. The workshop opened the participants' eyes to the possibility of considering a broader range of options, beyond the one with which they were most familiar. The discussion continued in community assemblies, including one in which a Spanish-speaking member of the Dudley Street Neighborhood Initiative in Boston shared their experiences.

Deliberations of the Housing Committee were rooted in six critical rights that were deemed to be indispensable for any instrument they might choose for controlling land, including:

- the right to stay put;

- the right to land tenure;

- the right to adequate housing;

- the right to property for individual residents;

- the right to benefit from improvements to the area; and

- the right to participate in the decision-making process and implementation of the District Plan.

Residents made a conscientious and audacious decision. They concluded that some form of collective land ownership was the only way to prevent gentrification and, despite the absence of any other CLT in Puerto Rico at the time, they concluded that a CLT would be the best option for enabling the Martín Peña communities to have control of the land. A community land trust would make possible the dredging of the Martín Peña Channel, the construction of needed infrastructure, and the rehabilitation of their neighborhoods, just as residents had envisioned in the Development Plan. The land was to be collectively owned in perpetuity, while each family who formerly lacked a land title would obtain a legal document — a surface rights deed — that would secure their right to use the land beneath their home, a right they would be able to bequeath to their legal heirs. This deed would enable them to stay put and to have a livelihood in the city, while securing their right to influence what might happen in their own neighborhood. They would no longer have to fear speculators, nor gentrification and involuntary displacement. With this decision behind them, they proceeded to secure the land and to initiate a new two-year participatory process to design how the first community land trust in Puerto Rico would manage its assets.

> They would no longer have to fear speculators, nor gentrification and involuntary displacement.

III. STRUCTURE AND FUNCTION OF THE CAÑO CLT

The Fideicomiso de la Tierra del Caño Martín Peña is a community land trust, constituted as a private, nonprofit organization created in perpetuity with an independent juridical identity. The Caño CLT is authorized to acquire land within and outside the Special Planning District, to develop and to sell housing (and other buildings), and to re-acquire these structural improvements, exercising a right of first refusal whenever owners desire to sell. The Caño CLT is entitled to create strategies and to design resale formulas which ensure the affordability of housing in perpetuity.

The CLT is a membership organization with an eleven-member Board of Trustees that is composed of community, private and government representatives, as follows: four

Trustees are Caño CLT members, whose homes are located on the lands owned by the Caño CLT; two Trustees are residents of the Martín Peña communities, designated to serve on the CLT's Board by the G-8; two Trustees are non-residents of the District, selected by the Board's members, based on skills and knowledge they can contribute to the CLT. The three remaining spaces are occupied by representatives of governmental entities, one from the Corporación del Proyecto ENLACE Board of Directors, one from the San Juan Municipality designated by the city's mayor, and one selected by the Governor of Puerto Rico.[7]

Caño CLT General Regulations

The legal grounds for the *Reglamento General para el Funcionamiento del Fideicomiso de la Tierra del Caño Martín Peña,* Rule 7587 (hereafter Caño CLT General Regulations), are the Puerto Rico Law No. 489, September 24, 2004, known as *"Ley para el Desarrollo Integral del Distrito de Planificación Especial del Caño Martín Peña"* (Law 489-2004), and the Puerto Rico Administrative Procedures Law. Through a democratic and participative process, a community committee was organized during 2006–2008. This committee gathered representatives from all seven communities who participated in several activities and workshops in order to establish the basis for the Caño CLT's General Regulations in accordance to the needs and concerns of Martín Peña communities' residents. The Caño CLT General Regulations were adopted on October 8, 2008, setting the regulations for the governance and operation of the Caño CLT and the rules and procedures for guaranteeing the administration of the land in favor of the communities' residents.

Law 489-2004 entrusted the Proyecto ENLACE Corporation with the constitution and promulgation of the Caño CLT's regulations. Law 489-2004 also defined the basic processes through which land would be identified and entitled to become part of the Caño CLT and established the framework for the Caño CLT to assign members to its Board of Trustees (23 L.P.R.A. section 5048).

The Caño CLT's General Regulations consist of fourteen articles which regulate the administrative aspects and the operational processes of the Caño CLT.[8] They define the organization's mission, vision, goals and objectives; the land trust's assets; the criteria to qualify as a member of the CLT; the rights of membership; the collaborative arrangements with ENLACE Corporation and the G-8; and other obligations and powers of the Caño CLT. Also, the Caño CLT's General Regulations carefully ensure community participation in all governing bodies within the project and decision-making processes. In order to ensure such participation, a Registry of Members is used to notify and summon Caño CLT members for activities such as assemblies, elections, and other deliberations, all convened after timely notification. The General Regulations also set standards and procedures for convening assemblies, establishing a quorum, and making announcements.

The Proyecto ENLACE Corporation, which was also created by Law 489-2004, is a governmental corporation created with a sunset provision. It is charged with the responsibility to advance the implementation of the Development Plan. The ENLACE Corporation and the Caño CLT converge in a multidisciplinary and multifaceted project called Proyecto ENLACE. These entities play complementary roles in achieving the goals of Proyecto ENLACE. The relations and interactions between them are established in the General Regulations, including how they work together to identify plots of land in the District, to plan new developments, and to allocate economic and human resources to achieve common goals essential to advance Proyecto ENLACE. Standards and procedures to address and review short- and long-term strategic plans and priorities for housing allocation are also delimited.

Aims and Objectives of the Caño CLT

The Fideicomiso de la Tierra del Caño Martín Peña was created to safeguard the land tenure and residential permanence of residents living in the seven neighborhoods along the Martín Peña Channel, while allowing and promoting development within the District. Among others, the aims and objectives of the Caño CLT were specified in Law 489-2004 as follows:

- Contribute toward the solution of lack of ownership rights of many Special Planning District's residents through collective title landholding;

- Address with equity the physical or economic displacement of low-income residents arising from gentrification, avoiding displacement and eradication of the communities;

- Guarantee affordable housing within the Special Planning District;

- Acquire and administer lands on behalf of and in the best interest of the community, increasing local control over the land, and avoiding absentee owner decision-making; and

- Enable the reconstruction and valuation of urban spaces.

Law 489-2004, and other regulations adopted in accordance to this Law, vested the Caño CLT with the authority and powers to accomplish these objectives.

Transferring Public Land to the Caño CLT

Following its participatory planning-action-reflection process, the community decided to adopt the community land trust ownership structure for addressing the lack of legal title among hundreds of families living on both sides of the Martín Peña Channel, families whose homes were located on public lands. This publicly owned land was to be transferred to the Caño CLT, all of which would be permanently owned and managed by the Caño CLT. Rights to individual parcels within the Caño CLT's landholdings would be conveyed to the families who were already living there through a durable surface rights deed for each parcel. These transfers and tenures united elements of Puerto Rico Civil Law and United States Common Law. This arrangement also incorporated the definition of the community land trust model found in amendments to the National Affordable Housing Act, passed by the U.S. Congress in 1992.

Elements taken from a civil trust model were the basis for transferring the public land to an entity controlled by the residents of the communities along the Martín Peña Channel through the Caño CLT. This transfer was constituted by the following components:

- The *settlor* who transfers the land, which in this particular case was the government of Puerto Rico;

- The *trustee* who receives ownership of the land with responsibility for possessing and administering it for the benefit of the communities, which in this particular case was the Caño CLT; and

- The *beneficiaries* who benefit from the administration of the land, which in this particular case were the residents who owned a structure on a portion of the land that was transferred to the Caño CLT.

Law 489-2004, Article 22, establishes that the corpus of the Caño Martín Peña CLT is comprised of all the lands transferred to the ENLACE Corporation for the purpose of creating the Caño CLT, as well as those acquired in the future in accordance with Law 489-2004. In addition, the Caño CLT was required to be governed according to the CLT General Regulations referenced above. Creation of such regulations were entrusted to the ENLACE Corporation.

The Caño CLT has an express limitation under Law 489-2004, forbidding the CLT from selling the public lands that were transferred to it. The Caño CLT is required by law to retain permanent ownership of the land. The Caño CLT is able to sell or to transfer rights over the edifices that are built on the land, however, and is also authorized to grant surface rights deeds and long-term leases, subject to hereditary rights. Homeowners who live on the once-public lands that were conveyed to the Caño CLT individually own their buildings, but they do not own the underlying land. The land is owned and managed by the Caño CLT for the common benefit of the Martín Peña communities, present and future.

Surface Rights Deeds

The transfer of public lands to the Caño CLT was mandated by Law 489-2004.[9] A majority of the government agencies that owned and controlled these lands at the time could not provide official documentation identifying the land registrar information, however; nor was there an official record of boundaries and value, making it difficult to proceed with transferring these public lands. This situation slowed down the work plan of the ENLACE Corporation.[10] To get a jump-start, volunteers for the Caño CLT made good efforts and identified registry information for some of the biggest parcels of land. Accordingly, a deed was authorized, specifying registry data for such properties.

The process of identifying and acquiring land is continuous, as the Caño CLT is constantly undergoing title investigations to identify parcels of land that may be transferred into its ownership. Currently, the Caño CLT owns and administers just over 110 hectares (272 acres) of land. Most of it (200 acres) was part of the original transfer of publicly owned land under Law 489-2004; another part of the CLT's landholdings (72 acres) was added gradually over the years as ENLACE acquired privately owned houses (with title to the land) to relocate homeowners directly impacted by the canal's dredging and then conveyed those parcels to the CLT.[11] All of this land, which is scattered throughout the seven neighborhoods of the Caño Martín Peña Special Planning District, is administered in the best interests of the Caño's residents, consistent with Law 489-2004, the District Plan, and the General Regulations.

One of the responsibilities of the Caño CLT is to identify those households who can benefit from a surface rights deed and to grant them such a deed in accordance with Law 489-2004. There are approximately 1,500 households living on the CLT's lands. To date, 110 surface rights deeds have been executed.[12] It is a slow and laborious process, since prior to executing the deed all documentation must be in place and the person or persons who appear on the deed must be the ones who have the legal right to do so.[13]

Through these surface rights deeds, the Caño CLT conveys individual property rights to those residents who own a housing structure on the Caño CLT's land. Homeowners possess the right to occupy and use the surface of the land beneath their homes, but they do not own the land itself. Generally, surface rights are granted in perpetuity or for a specific term. For its validity, surface rights are secured through public deeds that are then registered in the Puerto Rico Property Registry. After being officially registered, this legal instrument allows for two owners to co-exist in possessing separate portions of the same space: the Caño CLT owns the land and the resident owns the structure. The latter enjoys all the benefits of using, improving, and even mortgaging the surface right, as delimited by the Caño CLT in the surface rights deed.[14]

Publicly registered surface rights deeds specify the footprint under a resident's home, delineating the portion of land for which the right is granted. These deeds also identify the rights and obligations of the person to whom the surface right was conferred. Contained in the public deed, there is also a description

Fig. 5.4. Sixta Gladys Peña-Martínez, Caño CLT member and G-8 community leader, signing the surface rights deed for the land beneath her home, May 20, 2016.
MARÍA E. HERNÁNDEZ-TORRALES

of the housing structure. This is a legal requirement that allows the registration of the housing structure as a unit separate from the land. Other contents included in the surface rights deed are designed to protect houses on the CLT's land from non-mortgage or non-governmental debt claims under Puerto Rico's Safe Home Act.

The surface right's value amounts to 25% of the value of the plot of land on which a resident's home is located, becoming straightaway an asset for a family and increasing their wealth.[15] Surface rights can be inherited and mortgaged. Families can sell their surface rights, but not the underlying land. The Caño CLT retains a first right of refusal to purchase both the house and the surface rights whenever a homeowner decides to sell. By these means, the Caño CLT permanently holds title to the land and permanently controls the future disposition of the buildings located thereon, managing these assets for the benefit of the Martín Peña communities and future generations.

To the best of our knowledge, the Caño CLT is the first community land trust that has been used for the relocation of families, allowing for the construction of public infrastructure and following the parameters of the federal Uniform Relocation Act. Using a transfer of rights mechanism, the relocation process cost is reduced. Families can trade the houses in which they have been living — which, in most cases, are deteriorated and likely located on plots of land to which the families do not have a right — in exchange for a new house in better conditions, joining the Caño CLT and enjoying surface rights. The Proyecto ENLACE Corporation is in charge of the process of acquiring and building homes and relocating families.

IV. THE POTENTIAL FOR WIDER USE OF CLTs IN INFORMAL SETTLEMENTS

As of 2016, it was estimated that approximately 54.5% of the world's population lives in urban settlements; 828 million of these urban dwellers live in densely populated informal settlements, characterized by the lack of land tenure, inadequate and unsafe infrastructure, and insufficient sanitary installations (UN-Habitat, 2013: 112). In Latin America and the Caribbean, approximately 113 million people live in informal settlements (UN-Habitat, 2013: 127).

After almost a century of marginalization, the residents of the neighborhoods along the Martín Peña Channel, who had lived and struggled for decades with the collateral damage of living in an informal settlement, organized to create the Fideicomiso de la Tierra del Caño Martín Peña that is now working to overcome infrastructural, residential, environmental, and socio-economic deprivations and inequalities that accumulated over many decades.

The Caño CLT is an innovative, effective, and empowering organization that may serve as an example for other informal settlements around the world. Its potential for inspiring and informing land rights struggles in other countries was the reason for the

Caño CLT being internationally recognized by World Habitat in 2016. Since receiving a World Habitat Award, members of the Caño CLT have been widely sharing their experiences and instruments with community leaders in informal settlements in Latin American, the Caribbean, and South Asia, encouraging them to adapt the practices pioneered in San Juan to their own needs and contexts, possibly using a CLT to enable residents to gain secure use of land, to stop displacements, and to take control of local development.

Communities that are the most similar to the Martín Peña communities — and that have the greatest potential for adopting and adapting a Fideicomiso de la Tierra — are those that exhibit the following characteristics:

* A significant number of residents live on lands to which they do not have a valid or legal title for lands that may be owned by the government, by private individuals, or by a corporation. Alternatively, these lands may be occupied and used under some form of communal landholding system that has yet to be recognized and registered by the state.

* There are mechanisms available to acquire the land, including donation, adverse possession, purchase, or intervention by the state;

* A significant percentage of the population has a high sense of community cohesion and belonging; and

* The informal settlement is located within an area — or proximate to one — where land values are rising or where lands are coveted by speculative investors, threatening the present population with displacement.

The following ingredients have been essential to the success of the Fideicomiso de la Tierra del Caño Martín Peña. They should be considered by other communities when contemplating, planning, or attempting to create a CLT of their own.

Holistic Approach

The Caño CLT is part of a broader plan that was designed using a participatory process. This plan presumed that community organizations and inter-sectoral alliances would both be involved in its implementation. The plan itself included a multi-faceted focus on environmental justice, personal health, violence prevention, food sovereignty, young leadership, a solidarity economy, educational transformation, adult literacy, equitable relocation, quality public spaces, a right to the city, and securing land tenure and affordable housing in perpetuity.

Community Organization and Democracy

A CLT should be designed and developed through democratic processes promoting citizen participation, where citizens are the ones who identify their needs and priorities and who make decisions about the best ways to address these needs. For a CLT to be effective, communities must take part in the planning process and adapt the CLT to their context, needs, and expectations. Organizing and participation must continue even after a CLT has been created. Residents who live on a CLT's land and around that land must have a sense of solidarity and tranquility that comes from being part of an organization that protects their homes and interests. When asked to describe in one word what the Caño CLT means to her, Margarita Cruz, a resident of the Las Monjas community, said "Us. We are the Fideicomiso". A goal of every CLT should be to foster such a sentiment.

Capacity Building, Leadership and Skills Development

Popular education is a significant tool to achieve effective participation of communities. Community leaders should facilitate and promote the participation of residents in the activities of the community and in the design of participative strategies, ensuring that the needs and concerns of residents are heard and considered. Participatory processes are continuous and require capacity building and spaces for constant reflection.

Alliances

Professional support is fundamental. A multidisciplinary team of social workers, planners, urbanists, lawyers, architects, engineers, artists, and many more must work together with communities to advance and to execute a holistic plan. This kind of multidisciplinary team must value community knowledge, must promote critical thought, organization, and the exchange of knowledge between residents and professionals, and must stimulate alternate visions to understand local realities. By observing attentively and listening respectfully, outside professionals can respond to the community's agenda.

Multi-sectoral Associations

Community projects need the support of private and public sectors and academics in order to succeed. These associations expand the exposure of a community's struggles, giving more visibility, while also contributing technical knowledge and resources.

Legal Framework

It is necessary to pay close attention to the legal framework for the ownership and management of land, even if it means a community must create new instruments. Residents of the communities along the Martín Peña Channel examined different forms of land tenure, evaluating individual and collective options for owning the land. They decided on a community land trust, an innovative form of tenure never before used in Puerto Rico. Thereafter, new legislation was promoted in order to establish the Fideicomiso de la Tierra del Caño Martín Peña. The creation of Law 489 in 2004 was the result of an extensive dialogue among many knowledgeable people, but it was also the consequence of an intense political process.

Solidarity with Communities in
Other Countries Facing Similar Challenges

With the aim of sharing the strategies and instruments developed by residents of the Caño Martín Peña with other communities around the world, the Caño CLT is working on a new initiative called the "Espacio de Encuentro Internacional del Fideicomiso de la Tierra." This initiative will facilitate dialogue among community leaders, activists, academics, and politicians from countries and cities in the Caribbean, Latin America, Asia, Africa, North America, and Europe on collective, cooperative, and community-controlled forms of land tenure in informal settlements. It will also serve as an educational center and monitoring network, aimed at producing new knowledge about the creation of community land trusts and the effective participation of community residents in the equitable development and inclusive improvement of informal settlements. Through this initiative, the Caño CLT is now developing the logistics to spread the tools and instruments of the Fideicomiso throughout Puerto Rico and globally.

The Caño CLT convened an international peer exchange on April 29–May 4, 2019 in San Juan. With the title "Community Development and Collective Land Ownership," the Caño CLT gathered community members and residents from informal settlements around the world who are threatened with displacement or who anticipate such a threat in the near future. Community leaders from Argentina, Barbuda, Brazil, Belize, Bolivia, Chile, Ecuador, Jamaica, Mexico, Bangladesh and South Africa traveled to Puerto Rico. In every case, there was a representative from a community-based organization and/or from other allies who could support the development and organization of a CLT in their communities once they returned to their countries of origin.[16]

Participants shared experiences from their own communities and organizations. Many of their stories mirrored the experience of the Martín Peña communities, as participants reflected on the relevance of the Caño's struggle and trajectory for their own realities, identifying common factors in the struggles they face and finding similarities in their own journeys. They saw they have many things in common, even when they are from different countries. Strong bonds were established, based on similarity and solidarity. During the peer exchange and in feedback provided at the end, participants expressed how important it was to gather together and to realize that people are struggling with similar issues all around the world. They are not alone. They are stronger together.[17] It became clear that community organizing that provokes critical thinking and participation is central to addressing land tenure issues, particularly under a collective ownership regime.

CONCLUSION

A majority of CLTs in other countries have been established on lands that were vacant when acquired, allowing the construction of new homes; or CLTs have acquired vacant buildings and rehabilitated them. In both cases, these newly developed homes have been made available to a new group of low-income renters or homeowners. The Fideicomiso de la Tierra del Caño Martín Peña is different. It was created on lands where the homes of hundreds of families were already in existence and already occupied prior to creation of the CLT. "This CLT was born big," as residents often say.

The CLT developed by residents living in the seven Martín Peña communities provides a "proof of concept," demonstrating that CLTs can be an effective tool for regularizing land tenure in informal settlements threatened by displacement. A CLT can also provide for the redistribution of wealth and allow its members to gain control over a settlement's land, increasing their collective power.

The Caño CLT was developed by communities that experienced displacement firsthand, either by direct state action or by gentrification processes. It was designed to ensure that the much-needed environmental rehabilitation of the Caño did not result in the disappearance of the communities through increases in the value of the area's land. It was also born out of an aspiration for justice and equity, so that long-neglected communities and their residents would be the ones to benefit from a large-scale project they had long dreamed of, a project with the potential to transform both their neighborhood and the city.

Fig. 5.5. Mural in one of the Caño's neighborhoods, which reads: ". . . and for the first time we residents are creators of our own future." LINE ALGOED

As one of the late community leaders of the G-8, Mrs. Juanita Otero Barbosa, has said: "The Fideicomiso is the only salvation we have of continuing to exist and living in this community, so that they do not take us out of here" (Carrasquillo et al., 2009). In the current context, as the value of real estate in Puerto Rico is decreasing and as opportunities are soaring for speculation by outside investors who are buying up prime real estate all across the island, the Caño CLT has become increasingly relevant for the Martín Peña communities. Lands that used to belong to the government now belong collectively to the residents through the Caño CLT. These lands have been permanently removed from the market. There is no longer a risk of the government someday selling the land underneath the Martín Peña communities in order to monetize its value. As residents from the Martín Peña communities can often be heard to say, with pride and tenacity: "This land is ours, and nobody can take it away from us."

Notes

1. The Caño communities are: Barrio Obrero, Barrio Obrero Marina, Buena Vista Santurce, Israel-Bitumul, Buena Vista Hato Rey, Las Monjas, and Parada 27.

2. Puerto Rico is an archipelago in the Caribbean Sea. Besides the main island of Puerto Rico, there are two other important islands, Vieques and Culebra, as well as other keys and islets. For the purpose of this essay, we will refer to all of Puerto Rico as an "island."

3. This emigration estimate comes from the Center for Puerto Rican Studies at Hunter, City University of New York.

4. The other is the Voi-Tanzania CLT in Kenya, the subject of Chapter 14 in the present volume.

5. The Action Plan guides the use of the Community Development Block Grant for Disaster Recovery (CDBG-DR) allocated to Puerto Rico to cover the unmet needs remaining after emergency assistance and to mitigate risks.

6. The Cantera Peninsula community was a pioneer in elaborating its own comprehensive development and land use plan, adopted by the Puerto Rico Planning Board in 1995. Badly hit by hurricane Hugo on September 18, 1989, the first major hurricane that struck Puerto Rico since 1932, and as the reconstruction process was underway, residents realized their neighborhood was to be displaced for high end development projects. After partnering with others and organizing, in 1992 the Puerto Rico Legislature enacted Law 20 to create a government corporation that would work along with the community residents to rehabilitate the impoverished sector. The Cantera Community is not part of the Caño CLT, but the community leaders are part of the G-8.

7. Reglamento General para el Funcionamiento del Fideicomiso de la Tierra 2008, Art. V, sec. 2 (Caño CLT General Regulations).

8. These "general regulations" function much like the articles and bylaws that legally constitute most nonprofit organizations in the United States.

9. There are about 188 hectares (466 acres) of land within the Caño Martín Peña Special Planning District, but only the publicly owned land would be transferred to the Caño CLT, on which about 1,500 households were already living.

10. It is important to note that almost half of the residents at the Martín Peña communities have individual land titles as a result of clientelist practices of politicians, both at the state and municipal level. This means there are many instances where, comparing two neighbors on the same street, one might have had a land title conveyed by the government at a $1.00 cost to acquire the land underneath his or her home, while the other neighbor would remain without a land title. This practice endured for more than 30 years.

11. Most of the households who needed to be relocated to make space for the dredging have chosen to become members of the CLT have been provided with a new house and a surface rights deed.

12. This means that, as of October 2019, another 1390 households who are members of the CLT and who are living on lands owned by the CLT, were still waiting to receive their surface rights deed.

13. During the five years since 2014, the Caño CLT has received pro bono assistance from civil law notaries for the execution of these surface rights deeds.

14. 30 L.P.R.A. sec 6261-6276.

15. For persons who already owned and occupied houses on publicly owned land at the time it was transferred to the CLT, the CLT's board of trustees decided to award them a 25% share of the market value of the land underlying their houses. Should they later want to sell, the CLT will pay them that 25% of the land value. In the future, if the CLT develops new houses on land that it owns, a different policy may be put in place for these homes.

16. The peer exchange was divided into two sessions: one for Spanish and Portuguese speakers, gathering together fifteen international participants and participants from two communities in Puerto Rico; the other was for English speakers, gathering together thirty-one community leaders and representatives of community-based organizations.

17. During the peer exchange, an international conference was also held that was open to the general public, entitled "Recovery, Land Tenure, and Displacement: Perspectives from Grassroots and Community development." The conference discussed recovery initiatives after Hurricane María, land tenure issues in a global and local context, and the effects of gentrification that lead to displacement. Approximately 136 people heard about the Fideicomiso de la Tierra, followed by a dialogue with grassroots leaders from South Africa, Barbuda, and Argentina who talked about informality and threats to their homes and neighborhoods.

References

Algoed, L. and M.E. Hernández (2019). "Vulnerabilization and Resistance in Informal Settlements in Puerto Rico: Lessons from the Caño Martín Peña Community Land Trust." *Radical Housing Journal*, Vol 1(1): 29-47.

Algoed, L., M.E. Hernández Torrales, and L. Rodríguez Del Valle (2018). "El Fideicomiso de la Tierra del Caño Martín Peña: Instrumento Notable de Regularización de Suelo en Asentamientos Informales," Working Paper. Cambridge: Lincoln Institute of Land Policy.

Bonilla, Y. and M. LeBron (2019). *Aftershocks of Disaster: Puerto Rico Before and After the Storm.* (Chicago: Haymarket Books).

Carrasquillo, J., A. Cotté, V. Carrasquillo, and M. S. Pagán (2008). *Fideicomiso de la Tierra: Experiencias en el Proceso de Creación.* Escuela Graduada de Trabajo Social Beatriz Lasalle, Universidad de Puerto Rico.

Navas Dávila, G. (2004). "Fideicomiso social de la Tierra." Trabajo preparado para el Dr. Fernando Fagundo, Secretario de Transportación y Obras Públicas del Estado Libre Asociado de Puerto Rico.

UN-Habitat (2013). *State of the World's Cities 2012/2013.* Available from: *https://sustainabledevelopment.un.org/content/documents/745habitat.pdf* [Accessed 14 August 2019.]

UN-Habitat (2012). *Estado de las ciudades en América Latina y el Caribe, Brasil.* See also *Urban Development and Energy Access in Informal Settlements. A Review for Latin America and Africa,* ResearchGate. Available from: *https://www.researchgate.net/publication/309273730_Urban_Development_and_Energy_Access_in_Informal_Settlements_A_Review_for_Latin_America_and_Africa* [Accessed 25 Jul, 2019.]

6.

Community Control of Land
Thinking Beyond the Generic
Community Land Trust

Olivia R. Williams

No progressive housing pitch today is complete without a mention of community land trusts. CLTs have become a hot topic — especially in today's affordable housing crisis — because they decommodify land, taking it out of the speculative market so that no one can flip a house or build luxury condominiums on it.

The first CLT, New Communities, Inc., was designed by organizers from the Civil Rights Movement in the late 1960s as a mechanism for community control of land — especially for African-Americans in the rural South — in response to devastating rates of Black land loss.[1] The original CLT involved agricultural land, cooperative businesses, and plans for constructing four villages with new educational, recreational, and industrial systems to meet the needs of residents.

In the 1980s and 1990s, CLTs emerged in cities too, where they proved useful in reducing blight and providing stability in disinvested neighborhoods while providing affordable housing. Now, the model is often touted by many organizers as a "radical" way to secure community control of land and housing for the working class as prices go up, especially in the urban core of many American cities.

But when talking with hundreds of people in the CLT field across the United States while doing research on CLTs, it became clear to me that the CLT model is increasingly being perceived and promoted by housing advocates and practitioners as primarily an economically efficient affordable housing strategy, rather than an organizational approach that empowers poor, working-class, and marginalized people to take control of the land they occupy.

The creators of the CLT model intended for collective decision-making around site planning and development to be controlled by the users of the land, with a board of CLT trustees (some living outside of the CLT's land) acting to ensure that the land stayed affordable for generations. But as the model grew and proliferated, highly professionalized boards and staff started running the show in more and more CLTs without significant input from low-income residents and neighbors on what they needed in their neighborhoods.

One executive director from a CLT in Minnesota told me and my research team their thoughts about some of the old-time radicals at the early national CLT conferences:

> This is a business. This is about economic sense. I'm not drinking the Kool-Aid. You can't make me. I think you're all nuts that you're taking the commune kind of approach to life. That's not what we're about. We're about getting people into homeownership.

A staff person from another CLT, who responded to a question about community engagement initiatives in their CLT, said:

> It's about offering these opportunities [affordable homeownership] to more and more families who desperately need it. So we'll do whatever we can do to expand those opportunities. If it comes through some form of homeowner engagement, that's great, but we aren't reliant on that and we see it as a secondary issue.

These sentiments are not unusual among CLT practitioners in the United States. Even Grounded Solutions Network, the national organization for CLTs (which now promotes other housing strategies as well), has come to define its primary purpose as providing "permanently affordable housing." Most mainstream CLTs have become so narrowly focused on bricks-and-mortar housing production and the long-term stewardship of affordable housing that other uses and aspects of the model are often overlooked. As the ideal of community control has been erased from practitioners' internal dialogue and organizational mission statements, it has all but faded from practice.[2]

HOW DID THIS HAPPEN?

This has happened, in part, because CLTs face a common financial problem: the monthly lease fees (for the land) that are paid by CLT residents to a CLT organization are so modest — typically $25 to $50 per month — that they cannot sustain the organization. Theoretically, there's a point at which the number of housing units would be large enough to cover the basic costs of staffing and operating the CLT from lease fees alone. But the number of houses required to reach that break-even point — the "magic number," as some have called it — may be well into the thousands. Few CLTs have reached it. Most never will.

So, if an organization wants to sustain itself as a CLT, it has to bring in external grant money by actively pursuing new development projects on a rolling basis. In the United

> Dependence on external institutional sources of funding can make the goals of community control and non-housing development difficult to achieve.

States, the most readily available sources of grant funding for the development of affordable housing come from city governments, the housing trust funds administered by municipal and state governments, the federal government's Department of Housing and Urban Development (HUD), or private foundations. Most CLTs only stay alive by continually imploring these agencies and institutions for funds and by continually acquiring land and adding housing to their portfolios.

The increasingly competitive nature of most grants and the high price of land and housing development means that CLTs sometimes struggle to make ends meet. Often, CLTs find they are better off supplementing their affordable housing projects with a more profitable side-venture, so they also become a developer, lender, real estate agency, or the provider of other services to help pay for the operational costs of the CLT. This process of revenue diversification helps to ease the burden of the constant search for outside grants to operate the CLT, but it can also divert attention away from the needs of the most marginalized people in a community.

CLTs do important work in the context of rapidly rising land and housing values. They take property off the speculative market and hold it in perpetuity for low-income people. No developer can snatch up a plot of land once it is part of a CLT's portfolio. No real estate giant can develop that corner lot into luxury condos. The neighborhood around a CLT's holdings may become desirable, pricy, and gentrified, but CLT-held land will remain more affordable and accessible. This function of the CLT is what gets organizers and activists excited about the model, and for good reason.

But the dependence of CLTs on external institutional sources of funding can make the goals of community control and non-housing development difficult to achieve, since foundation and government funders tend to be most interested in encouraging CLTs to develop housing as quickly as possible. Financing the development of affordable commercial space, for example, can be more logistically challenging and financially risky than developing housing, so most CLTs stick to housing. Similarly, keeping CLT land undeveloped for the use of community gardens is not a lucrative use of valuable property, so that option is often rejected by CLT boards in favor of more housing.

Building affordable housing as prices rapidly rise is not *bad*, to be clear. But neighborhoods are so much more than housing. To radically change the way decisions are made about what we want our neighborhoods to be—and to create and maintain community-owned institutions and common amenities that are accessible—community land movements must look beyond the most common, generic ways that the CLT model is being operated, funded, and applied, seeking more independence from external funders.

FUNDER REQUIREMENTS:
A CASE IN POINT

In 2018, I was appointed to the Citizen Advisory Committee (CAC) in my city to oversee the distribution of Community Development Block Grants (CDBG), a federally funded program that allows cities and states to decide which local community development projects serving low-income people might be worthy of support. I saw the absurdity of a funder's requirements first-hand.

Every local government body that allocates CDBG funds is required to have a CAC, nominally to give localities more control over the administration of federal grants. In practice, sitting on the CAC felt like being a cog in the federal bureaucracy, a volunteer administrator checking boxes and adding up points, making sure all the prospective recipients of the grants we were distributing would fulfill their end of the agreement.

The resulting requirements are nearly impossible for small nonprofits to meet. For example, for an organization simply to purchase program supplies using CDBG funds, they must:

- Request a withdrawal of CDBG funds from the municipality;

- Buy the supplies within three days, write a justification for why the purchase took longer than three days, or return the funds;

- Produce and keep a purchase order or requisition form from an authorized representative of the organization;

- Keep an invoice from the vendor with a signature from the organization's representative, verifying the goods were received;

- Document where the supplies are stored;

- Document which objective(s) were fulfilled by the purchase of the supplies;

- Document which budget line item the supplies fall under; and

- Ensure that three separate individuals in the organization (1) authorize the transaction, (2) record the transaction, and (3) maintain custody of the goods purchased.

All of these requirements come after an organization has already written a detailed grant application meeting the objectives and checking the boxes required by HUD, including documentation of highly regimented accounting practices in their organization.

The regulations around CDBG allocations represent just one example of how the dominant paradigm of grant funding inhibits the autonomy of nonprofits. Private foundations can be just as cumbersome and biased in their grant stipulations. And, of course, only specific activities fall under the funders' goals. Federal money, for example, cannot be used for any "political activities." Private foundations, too, shy away from funding advocacy and organizing that are aimed at changing public policy and making governments more responsive to the needs of low-income and working-class communities, activities that are deemed "political."

THE RESULT: PROFESSIONALIZATION AND THE ABANDONMENT OF COMMUNITY ORGANIZING

In the old days, we had many conversations using the language of movement, about land reform, the importance of community control, and the fight for social justice. Community land trusts are, after all, children of the U.S. civil rights movement. But that language doesn't seem to surface much anymore, and the words we adopted to appease lenders, funders, and lawyers has become the internal language we use as well.

—Greg Rosenberg[3]

Funder requirements and restrictions like those I encountered in my own city are what earlier led the authors of *The Revolution Will Not be Funded* to argue for the abandonment of grant funding for nonprofit work.[4] Just the administrative burden of meeting the conditions of funders requires paid staff, office equipment, budgeting software, and professional skillsets beyond the capacity of many grassroots organizations. Once they grow to the capacity to handle grant applications and administrative tasks, many organizations find their original mission and goals getting gradually eroded or swiftly diverted to meet the requirements and priorities of their funders. The energy they once had for grassroots organizing gets channeled into bureaucratic work.

This argument is not new. Frances Fox Piven and Richard Cloward in their 1979 book, *Poor People's Movements: Why They Succeed, How They Fail,* made the case that "organizations endure, in short, by abandoning their oppositional politics."[5]

Many CLTs in the United States have followed suit, paring down their initial commitment to engaging, involving, and empowering the communities they serve in order to chase grant opportunities. There are exceptions of course, but CLTs with more radical ideals of community empowerment, community ownership of land, and anti-gentrification organizing tend to have a harder time finding the funds to fulfill their expansive, transformative missions.

Most public and private funders of CLTs are concerned primarily with the number of affordable homes that are being produced and preserved for lower-income people, not the ways that residents are engaged *after* they become the occupants of those homes, nor the needs that residents may have for non-housing development in their neighborhoods. CLTs that are serious about resident engagement often struggle to find the funds to support community organizing and any other kinds of non-housing activity.

The effect of funders' externally-imposed goals is particularly insidious considering how routinely and systematically low-income and marginalized communities are cut off from opportunities to assert their voice and agency in urban development. When improvements come to a low-income neighborhood, land values go up and can ultimately displace the population. Therefore, if you're poor, you're stuck between a rock and a hard place: live in blight or welcome new development and get kicked out of your neighborhood. For these reasons, CLTs can be important tools to bring improvements to neighborhoods, while insulating them from market speculation. Improvements *can* mean housing, but also so much more. When the market so inexorably limits marginalized communities' choices, it should be up to low-income residents to decide what they need in their neighborhood. Ultimately, CLTs can and should be vehicles of empowerment for people who are systematically disempowered. Indeed, this was the intention of the model's founders. Without this piece, CLTs lose a vital part of their legacy and marginalized communities remain voiceless in decisions about their neighborhoods.[6]

Paul Kivel's chapter in *The Revolution Will Not be Funded* encourages organizations to think about to whom they are accountable: their funders or a grassroots constituency in the communities they serve? He writes:

> In the nonprofit industrial complex, accountability is directed toward the ruling class and its managers — toward foundations, donors, government officials, larger non-profits, research institutes, universities, and the media. These are all forms of top-down accountability. I am suggesting a bottom-up accountability guided by those on the frontlines of grassroots struggles for justice. In which direction does your accountability lie?[7]

Most CLTs in the United States have become beholden to the goals of their funders, letting their missions drift away from some of the most radical pieces of the model's potential for impact. As a result, CLTs' accountability comes "down" from the stipulations of its funders instead of coming "up" from the preferences and needs of its community.

BEYOND GRANT FUNDING: POSSIBLE DIRECTIONS FORWARD

So how might a movement for community control of land and housing, which is where the CLT movement began, become more accountable to "those on the frontlines of grassroots struggles"? The challenges faced by CLTs today are primarily the result of two specific problems: the model's dependence on external funding, and the stipulations for receiving that funding.

Collective ownership of land *without* grant funding has long been proven possible, most notably in the cooperative housing field. Housing cooperatives have, for many generations, relied upon the capital of their founding members to acquire buildings *without* using external grant funding. But for low-income residents, finding the capital for a

> Maintaining participation must be an ongoing goal and practice of any community-owned land initiative.

downpayment on a building can be nearly impossible, and getting a group of people to commit to buying a building together can feel like a pipe dream.

Even when efforts to collectively buy property are successful at first, they are at high risk of failure if there isn't a backstop. Among housing cooperatives in the United States, close to half of all limited-equity cooperatives (LECs) eventually demutualize their assets; that is, their owners decide to sell either the entire building or their individual shares at market prices so that the co-op's units are no longer affordable.[8] For their part, group-equity cooperatives (independent group-owned houses) often run into legal and financial hurdles that undermine organizational sustainability, economic independence, and the development of additional housing.

Recognizing these challenges faced by housing cooperatives and the shortcomings inherent in the reliance of CLTs on grants from governments and foundations, there are new visionaries who are exploring community-funded models for the acquisition and ownership of land. Two examples: the East Bay Permanent Real Estate Cooperative[9] in Oakland, California and the Ecovillagers Alliance,[10] which already owns land and is starting a project in Lancaster, Pennsylvania. These are prototypes of collective ownership where non-resident members can invest in property that will still prioritize resident control of development and stay affordable for generations. The details of these models-in-development differ, but both of them involve different membership categories, including (residential and commercial) tenant members and investor members — and even individuals who choose to be *both* tenants and investors. With equity sourced from the community outside of the tenant pool, these organizations can grow without appeasing institutional funders for grant money to buy property, and they will be able to rely less on banks to finance property development.

Importantly, these two initiatives act as investment vehicles for people who want to pull their money out of ethically questionable markets and invest in affordable, sustainable, democratic land stewardship. Even tenants can build wealth this way by investing in cooperative land ownership and receiving dividends from the pool of rents collected on the land. They become tenants and landlords simultaneously, making decisions about their neighborhood's development collectively. Each tenant member gets only one vote in local decisions, no matter how much equity they invest. In terms of governance, tenant control is prioritized, with community investors having appropriately limited voting power.

CLTs can also experiment with and benefit from new strategies of community land investment. Homeownership-based CLTs by themselves tend not to generate enough revenue to repay a loan (even one sourced from the community). But in the right conditions, CLTs can find community financing strategies to be helpful in securing capital for site acquisition with revenue-generating community partners. The Oakland CLT, for example, has begun partnering with other community groups and cooperatives to purchase properties using community financing to keep commercial rent affordable for important community-based institutions in a rapidly-gentrifying city.[11] The Oakland CLT's vision for acquiring multiple community-financed sites in partnership with a set of mission-aligned local organizations may indeed light the way for other CLTs struggling with the tensions between grant funding and community control.

Because acquiring real estate requires considerable capital input as well as legal and financial knowledge, some degree of professionalism is necessary in all collective land-ownership strategies. The key is to combine that professional knowledge-base with an organizational infrastructure that fulfills the needs of marginalized communities, seeking as much of their leadership and input as possible. Maintaining a culture of participation and collective support must be an ongoing goal and practice of any community-owned land initiative, through social organizing, inclusive leadership, community-building activities, and partnerships with strong grassroots initiatives. While many CLTs find it difficult to be productive developers *and* sincere community organizers simultaneously,[12] some CLTs have managed to maintain organizers as full-time staff. And other CLTs partner with already-organized community groups to help them to attain the overall development and empowerment goals for their neighborhoods.[13]

THE SOCIAL JUSTICE CLT:
BACK TO BEING A MOVEMENT

This is a critical time in the movement for affordable land and housing. As real estate prices soar and wages stagnate, activists are seeking a way forward and often latch onto CLTs. But as Oksana Miranova has argued,[14] to address the housing crisis head-on, CLTs must be part of a comprehensive strategy involving rent control, public housing, and a network of other community ownership strategies. Organizers looking to keep land democratically controlled should be aware of the structural limitations of the CLT model and the limited funding environment we currently find ourselves in. Even if more funding sources are dedicated to CLT expansion, more CLTs will not necessarily mean more community-controlled development or grassroots planning efforts.

Without a continued focus on community control in CLTs, we lose opportunities to build and to cultivate multi-faceted CLTs with neighborhood amenities *beyond* housing. Admittedly, there are not as many clear funding sources or technical assistance providers for CLT applications and uses beyond housing. CLTs therefore find themselves pulled in the direction of housing development by their peer networks and grant providers, and the housing-focused CLT field perpetuates itself as a self-fulfilling prophecy. Those CLTs that have managed to develop community centers, playgrounds, commercial spaces, and urban farms — which they saw as important for their local communities — have done so by getting more creative with their budgets and funding sources. But nearly all of these CLTs have had to build their non-housing projects from scratch, without a guide to follow.[15] The result is that CLTs continue to be seen and funded primarily as an affordable homeownership tool.

For these reasons, I have highlighted a few new strategies for community-financed development focused on local needs and tenant control. Those of us who are passionate about democratic control of development must be willing to find creative ways to fund and to use CLTs, thinking beyond the usual applications that pull CLTs away from the communities they serve and away from the original intentions of the visionaries who brought the CLT into being.

Acquiring and administering property should not be the only goals of a movement for affordable housing and land. To confront the inequalities perpetuated by private property ownership — including deepening wealth disparities and the domination of urban development decisions by the elite — affordability must be coupled with bottom-up control of neighborhood development by residents. Somewhere along the road, the CLT movement largely abandoned this vital piece of its legacy. It is not too late, however, to reignite a passion and possibilities for community control.

Notes

1. New Communities, Inc., was subject to repeated discrimination by the State of Georgia, lenders, and insurance companies that put them in a difficult financial situation. They eventually lost their land in 1985 and won a settlement in 2009 that allowed them to purchase new property. See *https://www.newcommunitiesinc.com/about.html*.

2. There is ample evidence for this claim. See: J. DeFilippis, B. Stromberg, and O. R. Williams (2018). "W[h]ither the community in community land trusts?" *Journal of Urban Affairs* 40 (6): 755–69. Available at: *https://doi.org/10.1080/07352166.2017.1361 302*. Also see: B. Stromberg (2016). "Radical roots and pragmatic politics: The performance of land tenure reform in community land trusts." Doctoral dissertation, Rutgers University. Available at: *https://rucore.libraries.rutgers.edu/rutgers-lib/50192/*.

3. Greg Rosenberg was the long-time executive director of the Madison Area Community Land Trust and a founder and director of the National CLT Academy. He currently serves as co-director of the Center for CLT Innovation. For this reference, see Rosenberg, G. (2013). "Sell the CLT movement for what it is: radical and superior." *Rooflines: The Shelterforce Blog*. Available at: *http://www.rooflines.org/3389/ sell_the_clt_movement_for_what_it_is_radical_and_superior/*

4. INCITE! Women of Color Against Violence, ed. (2007). *The Revolution Will Not Be Funded: Beyond the Non-Profit Industrial Complex*. Cambridge, Mass: South End Press.

5. F. F. Piven and R. Cloward (1978). *Poor People's Movements: Why They Succeed, How They Fail.* Unknown edition. New York: Vintage. *https://www.penguinrandomhouse.com/books/131609poor-peoples-movements-by-frances-fox-piven-and-richard-cloward/9780394726977/.*

6. This argument is drawn in part from an earlier academic journal article: DeFilippis, B. Stromberg, and O. R. Williams (2018). "W(h)Ither the community in community land trusts?" *Journal of Urban Affairs* 40 (6): 755–69. Available at: *https://www.tandfonline.com/doi/abs/10.1080/07352166.2017.1361302?journalCode=ujua20.*

7. P. Kivel (2007). "Social service or social change?" In = INCITE! Women of Color Against Violence, ed. (2007). *The Revolution Will Not Be Funded: Beyond the Non-Profit Industrial Complex.* Cambridge, Mass: South End Press. pp. 129–150.

8. See UHAB (2016). "Counting Limited-Equity Co-Ops, Research Update." Available at: *https://www.uhab.org/sites/default/files/feb_update_for_website.pdf*

9. East Bay Permanent Real Estate Cooperative is organizing residents of the East Bay in California to cooperatively invest in, own, and develop mixed-use projects especially for marginalized communities of color. See *https://ebprec.org*

10. Ecovillagers Alliance is developing a replicable community land cooperative model that can be used to create affordable, mixed-use, urban retrofitted communities funded by community investors and linked to one another through regional or national networks through which equity can be transferred and shared. See *https://www.ecovillagers.org*

11. See O. P. Abello (2019). "A Worker Cooperative and a Community Land Trust Bought a Building Together." *Next City,* June 18, 2019. Available at: *https://nextcity.org/daily/entry/a-worker-cooperative-and-a-community-land-trust-bought-a-building-together*

12. The tensions and challenges that arise for CLT organizations doing development at the same time as community organizing have been detailed here: M. Axel-Lute and D. Hawkins-Simons. (2015). "Organizing and the Community Land Trust Model." *Shelterforce,* October 15, 2015. Available at: *http://www.shelterforce.org/article/4279/organizing_and_the_community_land_trust_model/*

13. For details, see: M. Axel-Lute and D. Hawkins-Simons (2015). "Community Land Trusts Grown from Grassroots: Neighborhood Organizers Become Housing Developers." *Land Lines,* July 2015.

14. See O. Mironova (2019). "How Community Land Trusts Can Help Address the Affordable Housing Crisis" *Jacobin,* July 6, 2019. Available at: *https://jacobinmag.com/2019/07/community-land-trusts-affordable-housing.*

15. See, for example, this thesis on the known US-based CLTs with commercial space, which summarizes the many different strategies and funding models the CLTs have used to secure commercial space in their portfolios: A. Curtis (2018). "Extending Community Control over Commercial Development: Community Land Trusts and Community Finance Models." Masters Thesis, Tufts University.

Acknowledgments

This article is a revised amalgamation of three previously-published pieces, listed below:

1. O. R. Williams (2019). "Community land without grants and debt." *Communities Magazine,* #182 Spring 2019. Fellowship for Intentional Community. Available at: *https://www.ic.org/community-bookstore/product/communities-magazine-community-land/.*

2. O. R. Williams (2019). "The problem with community land trusts". *Jacobin,* July 7, 2019. Available at: *https://www.jacobinmag.com/2019/07community-land-trusts-clts-problems*

3. O. R. Williams (2019). "Are we diluting the mission of community land trusts?" *Shelterforce,* August 30, 2019. Available at: *https://shelterforce.org/2019/08/30/are-we-diluting-the-mission-of-community-land-trusts/*

The CLT research and practitioners' quotes referenced in this essay came out of a collaborative research project that took place between 2014 and 2016 based on 124 interviews of stakeholders involved in eight CLTs in Minnesota. I want to acknowledge my CLT research team for the many hours of work they put into this project with me: Deborah G. Martin, Joseph Pierce, James DeFilippis, Richard Kruger, and Azadeh Hadizadeh Esfahani. This research was funded by the National Science Foundation BCS-GSS, grant #1359826.

7.

Better Together

The Challenging, Transformative Complexity
of Community, Land, and Trust

John Emmeus Davis

There is nothing simple about the community land trust. It is a complicated construct with many moving parts, all of which must work in concert for the CLT's unique approach to community-led development of permanently affordable housing on community-owned land to be done well. Its complexity is compounded by the fact that not every CLT is the same. The model's design is being continuously reinvented, giving rise to numerous organizational and operational variations.[1] These refinements have been crucial to the CLT's proliferation, helping it to adapt to a wide range of local conditions in a dozen different countries and to find acceptance among populations with diverse social, political, and economic interests.

The CLT's organizational and operational complexity is not merely a matter of the multiplicity and mutability of its constituent elements, however. The biggest challenge in mastering the model and making it sing lies in understanding that the whole is greater than the sum of its parts. It is the combination of community, land, and trust that contributes the most to a CLT's performance. The dynamic interaction of its three main components is what enables an organization to be a CLT and to behave like one.

Describing this complexity to people who are hearing about the CLT for the first time has never been easy. The most common technique employed by instructors like me has been to picture the CLT as a Venn diagram, where the model's principal components and essential concerns are depicted as three intersecting circles. "Community" is described in terms of a CLT's distinctive approach to involving residents of its chosen service area in guiding and governing the organization. "Land" is described in terms of the organization's distinctive approach to holding land forever, acreage that is scattered throughout a CLT's service area and conveyed via long-term ground leases to the owners of residential or commercial buildings. "Trust" is described in terms of a CLT's distinctive approach to the long-term stewardship of lands and buildings entrusted into its care, an operational

COMMUNITY
(Organization)

LAND
(Ownership)

TRUST
(Operation)

Fig. 7.1. Venn diagram depicting the "classic" community land trust.

priority that plays out in the programs of most CLTs through policies and procedures designed to preserve the affordability, quality, and security of heavily subsidized, privately owned housing.

This three-ring schematic has the advantage of simplicity. It allows a complicated model to be readily grasped in its entirety and then directs attention toward each component, inviting a closer examination of the key features and common variations that constitute the CLT's unusual treatment of organization, ownership, and operation. But simplicity can also have negative, unintended consequences. Indeed, I have come to suspect that our go-to image for illustrating and discussing what is widely known in the United States as the "classic" CLT may be inadequate at best and harmful at worst. It obscures too many of the complex interactions that invigorate the model. It overlooks too often the transformative potential of such complexity, as a CLT goes about its virtuous business of rebuilding a place of residence by restructuring the twin pillars of property and power.

Simplification is not only a problem for pedagogy but for practice as well. How a CLT is depicted has an effect on how it is implemented. Our attempt to cope with the model's messiness by stuffing it into three tidy circles on a static diagram means that we spend most of our time investigating the contents of each circle, while frequently failing to relate one circle to another. When that happens, when the interactions among the model's components are overlooked, we accidentally suggest that any one of them may be safely removed without damaging the whole. After all, if organization, ownership, and operation can be separately examined, they can be separately implemented — perhaps even discarded. Or so it would seem.

This occurs with distressing frequency in everyday practice. For example, a city government or non-governmental organization (NGO) may endorse a CLT's operational commitment to the lasting affordability of publicly subsidized, privately owned housing, while also embracing ground leasing as the most effective strategy for implementing and administering a stewardship regime. But the prospect of including a neighborhood's residents in planning a CLT's projects, in shaping its policies, and participating in its governance is considered an arduous, time-consuming annoyance. So this troublesome component is deleted from the start — or diluted along the way.

Another frequent occurrence: an NGO may behave like a CLT organizationally and operationally, engaging local residents in the guidance and governance of its activities while also providing a full complement of stewardship services, but the organization's leaders or funders decide to dispense with community ownership of the underlying land. Developing and financing affordable housing on leased land is deemed too difficult to do, so the CLT's bedrock commitment to owning land on behalf of a place-based community — and never reselling it — is set aside.[2]

This propensity for pruning cannot be attributed solely to the imagery that is commonly used in introducing the CLT. But when practitioners or funders who profess to support community land trusts do not hesitate in removing one or two of the model's main components for the sake of convenience, sawing off branches that have historically defined the CLT, it is fair to ask whether some of the blame for bestowing a license to lop should be assigned to the manner in which the model is described.

Perhaps the moment has come to find a different image to illustrate the CLT. If so, one option might be to substitute the dynamic mobile of Mr. Calder for the static diagram of Mr. Venn. I've been wondering of late whether it might be helpful, in other words, to portray the CLT as something akin to one of Alexander Calder's kinetic creations: a suspended apparatus that is finely balanced to turn freely in the breeze while remaining stably in place. *Community* would constitute one of the cross-pieces from which a variety of organizational configurations were hung. *Land* would be the second, balancing various interests of ownership. *Trust* would be the third, an operational strut to which were attached the multi-colored duties of stewardship, each festooned with weights and counter-weights all their own.

The best thing about this whimsical image of the CLT-as-mobile is that it cautions against the reckless removal of any component, lest the whole construct collapses. It also accepts as ordinary the real-world tensions that are intrinsic to community development. The artistry inherent in the construction of a mobile, like the artistry inherent in designing, constructing, and managing a CLT, lies in making a virtue out of necessity. Rather than pretending that interests are not in competition (and sometimes in conflict), the tensions that exist among various groups who share the same territory become the raw material for a creative endeavor that has as its greatest challenge and highest accomplishment a mastery of balance.[3]

A friend of Alexander Calder's, Saul Steinberg, once said of Calder that he was "a particular American type: the dogged tinker. We saw in him the face of a man who is always working on a perpetual motion machine, which he then sends to the patent office."[4] Mirrored in the image of the CLT-as-mobile, we find the faces of inventive practitioners engaged in a similar project. They are dogged tinkerers all, even if many of them are not American, as the model spreads to other countries. They are artistic realists who accept the challenge of finding the practical fulcrum at every point in a CLT's design. By their hands, the weighty concerns of "community," "land," and "trust" are adapted to the windy conditions within their own communities and kept stably, durably in balance.

Such a balancing act doesn't happen by itself. The CLT is a rather elegant model of community development, displaying a remarkable degree of adaptability and resiliency across a range of conditions, but it depends upon talented people to put it in place and to keep it aloft. Agency is as important as structure in fashioning and maintaining this perpetual motion machine. There are artists behind the art.

Much as I like this metaphor for describing how a CLT is built and behaves, however, I'm not quite ready to abandon the three-ring diagram that has long been used in trainings to depict the "classic" CLT. Yes, that familiar schematic has made it harder to appreciate the carefully balanced complexity of the model as a whole. Yes, it has made it easier to prune the model beyond recognition. But the fault lies less in Mr. Venn than in ourselves. Instead of substituting one metaphor for another, a more reasonable course of action would be for us to make better use of the imagery already in hand.

> More than the model's reinvention of each component, it is their combination that gives vitality, resilience, and power to a CLT.

We are not mistaken in picturing the CLT as a trio of interlocking circles; nor are we misguided in taking the time to understand, separately and thoroughly, the internal workings of the model's main components. Where we go wrong, I believe, is devoting too little attention to the spaces where the circles overlap. As a result, we tend to overlook the dynamic interaction of organization, ownership, and operation — and the delicate balance that must exist among them for a CLT to prosper.

These interactions are seldom discussed, rarely studied, and poorly understood. Such neglect is a major blunder, because the synergies produced by these interactions are what enable a CLT to perform to its highest potential. Organization and operation are made more effective by the innovative way in which a CLT's property is owned. The ownership and operation of a CLT's property are made more effective by the innovative way in which a CLT is organized. Ownership and organization are made more effective by the innovative way in which a CLT's lands and buildings are operated. More than the model's reinvention of each component, it is their combination that gives vitality, resilience, and power to a CLT.

Why go to all the trouble of identifying these interactions? What advantages would advocates and practitioners derive from a deeper understanding of the mutually reinforcing relationships among a CLT's main components? To my mind, they would possess a new set of tools for making their case. They would have at their fingertips a more compelling rationale for upholding the integrity of the CLT, which might stiffen their resolve in resisting the model's dismemberment. They would also have in hand a more robust measure for evaluating the model's performance, gauging when a CLT is working well and when it is not; providing them, too, with a finely calibrated scale for weighing whether a proposed adjustment to one of the model's main components is likely to preserve — or disrupt — the balance on which a CLT depends.

A few additional remarks about this balancing act. The particular genius of practitioners who are charged with implementing this unusual model of tenure, as suggested earlier, is their artistry in managing property-based interests that often compete — and sometimes conflict. CLT practitioners neither wish away these pesky tensions, nor regard their persistence as a sign of failure. They fashion them into something equitably in synch and sustainably in balance. Within the CLT's two-party structure of ownership, the ground lease is designed to balance the competing interests of the nonprofit landowner and those of the owners of any buildings located on the nonprofit's lands. Within the CLT's organizational structure, the two-part membership and three-part board are designed to balance the competing interests of the people who live on the nonprofit's lands and the neighbors who live around them. Within the model's operational structure, a CLT's stewardship regime is designed to balance competing priorities of enabling low-income households to gain access to homeownership and to build wealth in the present versus preserving that same homeownership opportunity for lower-income households in the future.

These difficult and daunting acts of balance are on daily display within the three-ring circus of a CLT. They capture our attention and win our applause. But we often fail to notice the other high-wire acts of derring-do that are being performed with quiet aplomb where the rings overlap. Here, too, CLT practitioners must skillfully balance competing interests and concerns.

There is an inherent tension, for instance, between the roles of CLT-as-developer and CLT-as-organizer. A CLT that tilts too heavily toward the former, giving too little weight to building a base of support within its service area, is unlikely to have the political clout to compete for land and money from its local government. It is unlikely to possess the legitimacy and loyalty that enables an organization like a CLT to surmount not-in-my-backyard opposition to its projects and to build local support for its unfamiliar form of tenure. Conversely, a CLT that tilts too heavily the other way, giving too much weight to every objection that might be raised by a vocal minority within its own service area or within its own membership, is likely to stumble in striving to acquire land, to assemble capital, and to develop affordable housing. Every CLT is forced to find a point of equilibrium, in other words, between building a substantial portfolio and cultivating an engaged constituency, maintaining a delicate balance between ownership and organization.

Another example. A community land trust that becomes too heavy-handed in carrying out its operational duties of stewardship can steadily undermine the "marriage of convenience" that must be maintained with the individuals and organizations that use its land. An imbalance in this pivotal relationship can increase the organization's costs, requiring constant intervention by the CLT to ensure that homes on its land are kept affordable, that buildings are kept in good repair, and that mortgages are paid. Conversely, a CLT that operates with too little oversight runs the risk of failing to fulfill its operational commitment to preserving the affordability, condition, and security of housing and other buildings entrusted into its care. There is a delicate balance between operation and organization.

Performing these feats of balance will always be a challenge. But the odds of success are greatly improved when practitioners appreciate on a deeper level the many interactions among a CLT's main components. There is a certain irony here. At the same time that practitioners are handed a stronger rationale for upholding the integrity of the "classic" CLT, they are allowed a wider latitude in modifying that model as needed. They are able to weigh with greater precision any proposed adjustments, watching closely to make sure their well-intentioned tinkering with the internal workings of organization, ownership, or operation does not throw their carefully designed construct completely out of whack. Practitioners who come to appreciate the model's interactive complexity discover that their license to lop has been revoked, but their freedom to improvise has been expanded.

> The transformative potential of a CLT is greatest when every part of this complex composition is present and performed in harmony with the others.

A deeper appreciation for the power of complexity also puts practitioners in the best position to bend the trajectory of local development toward justice. That is not to say that programs or policies that embrace less than the full package of the "classic" CLT are without merit. By itself, a community's ownership of land provides a platform for protecting access to goods, services, and homes for lower-income residents who might otherwise be extruded or excluded from a neighborhood. By itself, an organization's commitment to giving residents a voice in guiding development in their own locale and a role in governing the organization doing that development are marked improvements over top-down approaches to neighborhood revitalization. By itself, an operational commitment to the lasting affordability of housing, secured through a watchful stewardship regime, is a vast improvement over policies and programs that allow affordably priced homes produced through public dollars or private donations to leak away. Each reinvention of organization, ownership, and operation has value; each helps to make place-based development more equitable in the short run and more sustainable over time. But two components are better than one, and three are best. The transformative potential of a CLT is greatest when every part of this complex composition is present and performed in harmony with the others.[5]

At the risk of trotting out one metaphor too many, let me end with a story that predates my personal involvement with community land trusts. Nearly fifty years ago, I spent summers in the mountains of southern Appalachia, doing community organizing as a member of a project called the Student Health Coalition.[6] One of my fellow organizers, who was eager to immerse himself in Appalachian culture, managed to persuade a retired coal miner to give him weekly lessons in playing the country fiddle. My friend was a quick study in mastering the instrument's fingering because he already played the guitar. He had a harder time making the fiddle sing, however, as he sawed clumsily across the strings. Exasperated by his pupil's lack of progress, the gray-haired fiddler would interrupt their sessions again and again with the same admonishment: "Charles, any damn fool can figure out where to put his fingers. The music is in the bow, boy; the music is in the bow."

Faced with the challenge of teaching people to play an instrument as demanding as the CLT, I am frequently reminded of the old fiddler's advice. Whether introducing the model to a new audience or bringing the model to a new venue, the first lessons must always be focused on getting the fingering right within the separate spheres of ownership, organization, and operation. A novice must have a basic command of each component before tackling more difficult exercises. But that will never be enough to coax a compelling tune from a CLT. Any damn fool can figure out where to put his or her fingers, sliding along the taut strings of organization, ownership, and operation. Mastery of the model only comes when they are played in combination. It is here, among the complex harmonies of *community, land* and *trust*, that a song of transformation is most likely to be heard in the places people call home. The music is in the spaces, boys and girls; the music is in the spaces.

Notes

1. These variations extend to the manner in which the CLT itself is characterized. Many practitioners employ terms like "strategy," "mechanism," "vehicle," or "platform" when describing the CLT. I have done the same, sometimes using these terms interchangeably with "model." My use of the last is not meant to champion model as the best of these terms. It is merely to follow the custom that began in 1972 with the first book about the CLT, which called it "a new model for land tenure in America."

2. This is hardly the first time I've bemoaned (and ridiculed) the readiness to discard this component of the "classic" CLT whenever funders, bankers, or practitioners consider community landholding and long-term ground leasing to be "too difficult." See, for example: "Ground Leasing Without Tears," *Shelterforce Weekly,* January 29, 2014. Available at: *https://shelterforce.org/2014/01/29/ground_leasing_without_tears/*

3. An early attempt to develop a theory of the formation and interaction of these "property interest groups" can be found in J.E. Davis, *Contested Ground: Collective Action and the Urban Neighborhood* (Ithaca, NY: Cornell University Press, 1991).

4. Adam Gopnik, "Wired: What Alexander Calder Set in Motion." *The New Yorker* (December 4, 2017: 73–77).

5. A more detailed argument for the transformative potential of the "classic" CLT can be found in J.E. Davis, "Common Ground: Community-Owned Land as a Platform for Equitable and Sustainable Development." *University of San Francisco Law Review* 51 (1), 2017. Thoughtful critiques of this argument, addressing the question of whether nonmarket models of ownership are, in fact, "politically transformative," appear in James DeFilippis, *Unmaking Goliath: Community Control in the Face of Global Capital* (Routledge, 2004) and his more recent essay, "On the Transformative Potential of Community Land Trusts in the United States," co-authored with Olivia R. Williams, Joseph Pierce, Deborah G. Martin, Rich Kruger, and Azadeh Hadizadeh Esfahani. *Antipode* (February 12, 2019).

6. An online archive of materials about the Appalachian Student Health Coalition is part of the Southern Historical Collection at the University of North Carolina (*www.coalition.web.unc.edu*).

ABOUT THE CONTRIBUTORS

LINE ALGOED is a PhD researcher at Cosmopolis, Center for Urban Research at the Vrije Universiteit in Brussels and a Research Fellow at the International Institute of Social Studies in The Hague. She works with the Caño Martín Peña CLT in Puerto Rico on international exchanges among communities involved in land struggles. She is also an Associate at the Center for CLT Innovation. Previously, Line was a World Habitat Awards Program Manager at BSHF (now World Habitat). She holds an MA in Cultural Anthropology from the University of Leiden and an MA in Sociology from the London School of Economics.

JOSHUA BARNDT is Executive Director of The Parkdale Neighbourhood Land Trust, a nonprofit, community-based organization that acquires land for affordable housing, supportive housing, and community economic development in Toronto's Parkdale neighborhood. He is a co-founder of the Canadian Network of Community Land Trusts. He previously worked as Community Liaison Officer coordinating a community benefits agreement as part of the Lawrence Heights Revitalization. Earlier, he served as Communications and Campaign Consultant for the "Right to the City Alliance" in New York City. He holds an MS in Design and Urban Ecologies from the Parsons School of Design, The New School.

SUSANNAH BUNCE is an Associate Professor in the Department of Human Geography at the University of Toronto Scarborough, Toronto, Canada. She has researched community land trusts in cities since 2009 and was the principal investigator on a three-year research project that examined urban community land trusts in Canada, the United States, and the United Kingdom, funded by the Social Sciences and Humanities Research Council of Canada. Her research on CLTs has been published in international academic journals and in a recent monograph published by Routledge. She holds a MES Planning and PhD in Environmental Studies from York University, Toronto.

JOHN EMMEUS DAVIS is a founding partner of Burlington Associates in Community Development, a national consulting cooperative. He was housing director in Burlington, Vermont under Mayors Bernie Sanders and Peter Clavelle. Community land trusts have been a prominent part of his professional practice and scholarly writing for nearly 40 years. His publications include *Contested Ground* (1991), *The Affordable City* (1994), *The City-CLT Partnership* (2008), *The Community Land Trust Reader* (2010), and *Manuel d'antispéculation immobilière* (2014). He co-produced the film, *Arc of Justice,* and is co-director of the Center for CLT Innovation (*https://cltweb.org*). He holds an MS and PhD from Cornell University.

ALAN GOTTLIEB is a Colorado-based writer, editor, journalist, and nonprofit entrepreneur with more than 20 years of experience in education policy and education journalism. Currently, Alan is owner of Write.Edit.Think.LLC, an independent communications consulting firm. Alan co-founded Chalkbeat, a growing and increasingly prominent national news nonprofit focused on PreK-12 education policy, policy implementation and practice. From 1988-97, he was a reporter and editor with *The Denver Post.* From 1997 until June 2007, he served as education program officer at The Piton Foundation in Denver. He is the author of two books, one fiction, one non-fiction.

MARÍA E. HERNÁNDEZ-TORRALES holds an LLM in environmental law from the Vermont Law School and an MA in Business Education from New York University. She studied for her undergraduate and Juris Doctor degrees at the University of Puerto Rico. Since 2005 she has been doing pro bono legal work for the Proyecto ENLACE and for the Fideicomiso de la Tierra del Caño Martín Peña. Since 2008, Hernández-Torrales has worked as an attorney and clinical professor at the University of Puerto Rico School of Law where she teaches the Community Economic Development Clinic.

AARON MIRIPOL is a leader in nonprofit real estate development with a focus on growing CLTs for the benefit of local communities. Since 2007, as President of the Urban Land Conservancy, he has overseen 38 investments in Metro Denver, including multi-family affordable housing, schools, and commercial space. Prior to ULC, Aaron led Thistle Community Housing, increasing its portfolio from 100 to 1,000 permanently affordable homes, including 250 for-sale homes. In his career, Aaron has overseen $800M in affordable housing and community development. He gained an early appreciation for CLTs while working at Moshav Kerem Maharal, a cooperative farm in Israel.

TONY PICKETT is Chief Executive Officer of the Grounded Solutions Network, advancing a racial equity agenda to increase the scale and impact of shared equity housing with lasting affordability. His career spans over 35 years, including LEED Accredited

Professional work as a commercial architect and affordable housing developer. His expertise includes CLT financial business planning/modeling. He is a member of the Center for CLT Innovation's advisory committee and a co-author of "Community Land Trusts: Combining Scale and Community Control to Advance Mixed-Income Neighborhoods," an essay published by Case Western Reserve University. Tony holds a BA in architecture from Cornell University.

LYVIA RODRÍGUEZ DEL VALLE is the former Executive Director of the Caño Martín Peña CLT and Corporación Proyecto ENLACE del Caño Martín Peña. For over 15 years, she worked with an interdisciplinary team and community organizations on implementation of the ENLACE Project. Lyvia previously worked on urban revitalization in San Juan and risk management and decentralization in Quito and Asunción. She holds a master's degree in Urban and Regional Planning and a graduate certificate in Latin American Studies from the University of Florida, Gainesville, and a bachelor's degree in Environmental Design from the School of Architecture, University of Puerto Rico.

EMILY THADEN is the Director of National Policy and Sector Strategy for Grounded Solutions Network (GSN) where she has worked since 2011. She leads GSN's work to increase financing and funding for shared equity homeowners and programs and develops innovations to expand permanently affordable housing opportunities. Previously Emily developed a shared equity program in Nashville, Tennessee. She is currently the Vice Chair of the board for Nashville's housing authority, the Metropolitan Development and Housing Agency. She is also Vice Chair of the board for *Shelterforce*. She received her doctorate in applied community research from Vanderbilt University.

BRENDA M. TORPY helped to create the Burlington CLT, now the Champlain Housing Trust, in 1984, while serving as Burlington's Housing Director under Mayor Bernie Sanders. She has been executive director since 1991. CHT is currently the largest CLT in the USA, with 3,000 homes, and won a United Nations World Habitat Award in 2008. Brenda was a Ford Foundation Leader for a Changing World in 2002. She is on the board of Grounded Solutions and on the advisory board of the Center for CLT Innovation. She was a past member of the Boston Home Loan and Federal Reserve Banks' advisory committees.

KARLA TORRES SUEIRO (ktorressueiro@gmail.com) is a lawyer specializing in socio-economic and citizenship rights. She is a Staff Attorney at the ABA Pro Bono Asylum Representation Project, providing legal representation for unaccompanied children in immigration detention at the south Texas border. Karla previously assisted with appeal cases from EU citizens in the UK who were exercising their rights of citizenship and residency. She joined the Caño CLT in 2016, where she helped to manage the worldwide exchange of knowledge about forms of collective land tenure. She holds an LLM in International Criminal Justice and Human Rights from the University of Kent.

OLIVIA R. WILLIAMS is an independent scholar and organizer living in Madison, Wisconsin. She received a PhD in Geography in 2017 from Florida State University with research on community land trusts. She currently serves on the staff of the Madison Area CLT and the Madison Community Cooperative. Olivia also works to sustain and promote group-equity housing cooperatives through her board service at North American Students of Cooperation Development Services and is actively developing a new model of community land investment and ownership called the community land cooperative (CLC) with the Ecovillagers Alliance.

www.ingramcontent.com/pod-product-compliance
Lightning Source LLC
Chambersburg PA
CBHW080713050426
42336CB00062B/3246